THE
WACKY
CHRISTIE
TRIAL

BY HARRY HARRIS

EMPIRE
PUBLICATIONS

First published in 2022

EMPIRE PUBLICATIONS
1 Newton Street, Manchester M1 1HW
© Harry Harris 2022

ISBN: 9798835242801

ACKNOWLEDGEMENTS

Many thanks to Alan Edwards, one of the top PR's of his generation who actually knows Posh & Becks having represented them, for his insight into the celebrity couple.

I am also indebted to Martin Townsend, the former Editor of *OK magazine*, providing his inimitable insight into the Beckhams, having been instrumental in signing their £1m deal with the magazine, and he now works in PR as a leading media expert with Pagefield.

Thanks also to Norman Giller who wrote *Billy Wright - A Hero for All Seasons* for his insight into the first football celebrity couple Billy Wright and Joy Beverley of the Beverley Sisters.

Thanks as always to John & Ash at Empire Publishing in Manchester, most definitely not a celebrity WAG couple!!

INTRODUCTION

When Gareth Southgate comes to name his final squad for the World Cup in Qatar, he will have taken note of the extraordinary revelations that emerged in what has been dubbed the 'Wagatha Christie libel trial'. You'd be forgiven for thinking that he will need to speak to Harry Kane's missus as well as the England captain to ensure that he has the right personalities for the task in the Middle East, and not just on the playing field, but also behind the scenes where the WAGS can have such a devastating and disruptive influence.

Perhaps a chat with Roy Hodgson and Gary Neville will shed more light on the WAGs (Wives and Girlfriends) role in World Cup and European Championships, the full extent of their antics only now coming to light when Rebekah Vardy sued Coleen Rooney, and the former England captain gave evidence in front of the Vardys with Jamie squirming on the bench in his seat in London's High Court wondering whether the absence of a call from the England manager asking him to reconsider his decision to retire early from international football is down to more than just football criteria. Since announcing his international retirement in 2018 Vardy has notched 75 times for Leicester in all competitions but despite a clamour from pundits and press Southgate showed no inclination of picking the in form striker for Euro 2020. Perhaps the England boss will have remembered the behind the scenes disruption caused by his wife and thought twice about bringing Vardy back into the England dressing room?

The trial burst into life when Vardy left court early with his wife and hit out at fellow England international Wayne Rooney for 'talking nonsense' following a claim that the then England manager Roy Hodgson had asked Rooney to tell Vardy to get his wife to 'calm down' during Euro 2016. The spat caused a social media frenzy as you would expect. Euro 2016 was a really poor tournament for the three lions on and off the pitch – England were humiliated and dumped out of the competition by minnows Iceland, while the shadow of widespread football violence hung over much of the tournament - now we discover that behind the scenes the team was disrupted, perhaps even distracted, by Rebekah's meddling media activities.

The press galleries were packed for Wayne Rooney's much-anticipated appearance in court. An indication of his nervousness came as Wayne knocked into a table, sending water spilling all over it, with his wife leaping to his rescue to mop up the mess. It won't be as easy for the

Vardys to sort out their mess, though. To be fair to Wayne, he has been in court every day, holding his wife's enormous bag, no doubt filled with court papers and Coleen's copious note taking during the trial. Jamie, however, turned out just the once, no doubt to hear what Wayne had to say, and it didn't make for comfortable listening.

The then England captain said he was pulled aside by Roy Hodgson and assistant Gary Neville and asked to raise the 'awkward' issue with Vardy over concerns that Rebekah was 'causing problems and distractions' for the team but Vardy was quick to dismiss the allegation claiming that the conversation with him never happened. When told that Jamie denied he was asked to get Rebekah to 'calm down', Rooney said: 'I'm sat here on oath. I 100 per cent spoke to Mr Vardy. If he wants to say that and relay that back to his wife that's entirely his business.'

But in a statement issued by Vardy's representatives outside the hearing, the Leicester City star said: 'Wayne is talking nonsense. He must be confused because he never spoke to me about issues concerning Becky's media work at Euro 2016. There was nothing to speak about, I know this because I discuss everything with Becky.'

Shortly after issuing the statement, Rebekah and Jamie left the court early in an afternoon break claiming that Rebekah was feeling ill. One of Rebekah's barristers, Sarah Mansouri, apologised to Mrs Justice Steyn for their absence for the rest of the day, saying they meant 'no disrespect'. The court heard Rebekah's claim that Vardy was never given such a message by Rooney - and she even said that she had raised the matter with Rooney during one of her FaceTime conversations with Vardy at Euro 2016.

However, Rooney said he did not recall being next to Vardy when he was having a conversation with Rebekah, in which Rooney is alleged to have denied the conversation took place.

And Rooney added that he did not know whether Vardy had told his wife that Hodgson had asked Rooney to speak to Vardy about her.

Rooney told the High Court in London: 'They asked me, as captain, would I be able to speak to Mr Vardy on issues regarding his wife and I think we all knew we spoke about it, it was an awkward subject.' Rooney, 36, said he asked him to 'ask his wife to calm down and not bring any issues off the field that were unnecessary.'

Rebekah's lawyer Hugh Tomlinson QC asked him: 'Ask his wife to calm down - she wasn't dancing on tables?' Rooney said: 'No, I wasn't aware of that. It was a lot of negativity amongst a lot of media coverage which as a group of players and as the manager of England he didn't want that to happen, so he asked would I be able to speak to Jamie and I went and done so.'

Among the issues was the idea Rebekah had 'some kind of column in *The Sun*', the court heard. Rooney added: 'I think there was a few things at the time with Rebekah which the leaders of the team asked me to speak to Jamie about. I was of the understanding that Rebekah had a column in *The Sun* newspaper and as I state... I obviously had better things on my mind. It was obviously awkward for me.'

Rooney added that there had been negative media coverage, saying: 'I was asked to speak to Mr Vardy by the England manager and I carried out that instruction. It was an awkward situation for me and I'm sure it was an awkward situation for Mr Vardy, but I felt it was in the best interests of the team.'

Euro 2016 was another crack at ending all those years of heartache without a trophy since The Boys of 66. Before the tournament, Rebekah Vardy had told the London Evening Standard 'my main concern is to be there to support Jamie, as his wife... It's to be there to support him, not to join a fashion parade.' But the evidence at the High Court appeared to tell a very different story as her media meddling was brought to the attention of the mild mannered England boss, Roy Hodgson and managed to test even his patience to the extent that he felt forced to call in his skipper to keep the WAGs in check.

The WAGs had caused trouble 10 years earlier at the 2006 World Cup in Germany when they took over the pretty German spa town of Baden

Baden. In their ranks back then was 20-year-old Coleen, then just a promising youngster in a star-studded squad led by the self-styled queen of the WAGs, Victoria Beckham. The 2006 vintage went on a spectacular one-month parade, designer shopping by day, partying by night. 'They were lipstick ladettes who swore like dockers, partied like rock stars and dressed as if they were on their way to a strippers' convention in Las Vegas,' observed Daily Mail columnist, Jan Moir. It was bad luck for the boys as the WAGs made more impact off the field than England managed on it in Germany. Eriksson's team lost in the quarter finals to Portugal on penalties and the sideshow was described as a 'circus' by England defender Rio Ferdinand, that he hoped would never be repeated. Some hope!

At the 2010 World Cup in South Africa, England's Italian hard-line coach, Fabio Capello, wanted nothing to do with the WAGs and let his players know how he felt. But Capello went too far, and as England's Golden Generation failed once again, it was claimed the players had been bored and isolated at their remote South African training facility and the cry among press and public was 'bring back the WAGs!'

Back they came with a bang, in every sense. In 2016, the WAGs were back but with certain limits imposed by manager Hodgson. They were banned from the £900-a-night Auberge du Jeu de Paume hotel in the grounds of Chateau de

Chantilly, where the England squad was based, however rendezvous between players and partners were sanctioned after matches, with stars chauffeured to the luxury villas dotted across the French countryside where their loved ones were billeted. Rebekah had married Jamie at a lavish ceremony at the exclusive Peckforton Castle in Cheshire a month before the tournament began - the star-studded guest list for their reception included One Direction's Louis Tomlinson, rapper Tinchy Stryder and Kasabian frontman Serge Pizzorno. The couple were quickly dubbed the 'new Posh and Becks' and the party was splashed across the pages of Hello! Magazine, in itself oneupmanship from Posh and Becks wedding splash in *OK magazine*!

The WAGs were still in party mood by the time they got to France; wearing England shirts with their name emblazoned across the back. Jamie was one of England's big hopes after a spectacular season with Leicester, and he didn't seem to mind too much what his new wife got up to; the famous football honeymoon period was still in play. Now it was also about your social media stats - Coleen, already a veteran of major tournaments, had accumulated 1.24million Twitter followers and a further 320,000 on Instagram by the time the tournament began.

Up in the stands at Lens for England's second match, a 2-1 win over Wales, Rebekah performed an admirable man-marking job on

Coleen worthy of Alan Mullery's shadowing of Pele in Guadalajara in 1970. 'The seat that Rebekah was sat in during the game on 16 June 2016 was not her allocated seat,' FA family liaison officer, Harpreet Robertson, explained in a written statement to the court. Rebekah 'wanted to be sat in the seats that were right in the eye line of anyone looking at, or photographing, Coleen,' added Robertson. Rebekah denied the claim, saying Ms Robertson 'took an immediate dislike to her'. 'I find it quite interesting,' Rebekah told the court. 'I think it's nonsense, absolute nonsense.'

However Rebekah did indeed up end sitting right behind Coleen, thereby in direct camera shot for that toothy smile when images were taken during a game in which Jamie scored the equaliser before Daniel Sturridge hit the winner in injury time. Rebekah can be seen celebrating with Coleen as England notched their only win of a poor tournament. 'Her behaviour during the game suggested to me that her focus was little or nothing to do with the football match,' Robertson recalled. 'I remember that Rebekah was constantly on her phone, often taking selfies and generally showing very little interest in the match itself.'

The seat rumpus prompted 'security concerns', according to the FA officer, and ended in an altercation with Rebekah's guests that 'almost reduced me to tears', said Robertson. 'I asked them to move but they refused and were incredibly rude and abusive to me, remarking words to the effect of "we can sit where we like, f*** off".'

It was clear that Rebekah was building her own social media empire when she tweeted from Marseille, where England played Russia on June 11. English fans clashed with French police the day before the game, fights broke out with Russian supporters after the match, which finished 1-1 when Russia scored a 91st-minute leveller.

'In the carnage with England fans,' tweeted Rebekah, clutching a pint of lager.

Then Rebekah criticised the French authorities, which would have troubled the England management: 'Teargassed for no reason, caged and treated like animals! Shocking.'

Rebekah was documenting her personal tournament in a column for *The Sun* and in various TV interviews, while FaceTiming her new husband so frequently, according to evidence given in court, that the other players felt she was there with them at the Auberge du Jeu de Paume.

With his team needing a win against Iceland in England's first, and as it turned out so disappointingly, only, knockout match, England boss Hodgson and his assistant, Gary Neville, who is now Sky pundit, had to stop the WAGs antics so sought out captain Rooney to talk to his teammate Jamie. Wayne disclosed that the England players agreed before the tournament that they didn't want any 'distractions'. 'We didn't want any newspaper columns,' he told the court. With Rebekah and Jamie sat in front of him in court, Wayne described in graphic detail how his difficult conversation with Jamie and his now famous line about how he wanted his team-mate to tell his misses to 'calm down' took place over a Red Bull and a coffee at the team hotel.

During the tournament a story leaked out of the England camp as The Times reported that 'the captain and other senior players have spoken to Jamie Vardy about the prominence of his new wife, Rebekah, in the media'. England emerged from Group B at Euro 2016 following a 0-0 draw with Slovakia, but the story prompted questions to the England captain at a press conference on the eve of England's round of 16 match against Iceland. Hodgson jumped in: 'I will answer for Wayne. There are no problems between Wayne Rooney and Jamie Vardy. They are good friends and this is a salacious story that has been spun.'

Having covered four World Cups for the Daily Mirror as their chief football writer, there have been times I have discovered inside information from within the England camp and duly reported it, only for the story to be 'knocked down' in formal press conferences. Eager journalistic rivals eager to toe the party line relish knocking down a rival's exclusive. Yet, years later, when the truth finally emerges in a player's autobiography, it turns out the story was right in the first place. Here it was no different. It was the England manager's job to put a lid on such speculation about internal rifts which clearly had an effect on team spirit. Whether that had anything to do with England's humiliating defeat at the hands of the fishermen and carpenters of Iceland remains a matter of conjecture. The shock 2-1 defeat was described by Gary Lineker as 'the worst defeat in our history', the former England striker adding that Iceland has 'more volcanoes than professional footballers'.

The 2018 World Cup saw the WAGs back in action, and it seemed like they had never been away! It was arguable that in some ways they were worse with Rebekah accused in court of tipping off a newspaper photographer when they all ate at a restaurant at the 2018 World Cup in Russia which left many of the WAGs 'absolutely devastated' that they had been set up. One said she 'could not believe' the suggestion that a fellow WAG would even consider 'doing the dirty' on them in such a way.

New boss Gareth Southgate had won the trust of the players but now, following Wayne Rooney's retirement from international football, Rebekah took centre stage, going from reality TV contestant to being hailed 'Queen WAG' by the press - with branding experts claiming she was a 'natural fit' to take the crown from Coleen.

Eager to maximise her status, Vardy set up publicity shots outside a restaurant in St Petersburg, where she had invited other WAGs to dine, according to FA liaison officer Robertson. But times were changing under Southgate, the more established WAGs were not keen to be 'papped'. Robertson claimed Rebekah had only invited the younger women to the meal. She wrote in her statement: 'I recall being informed by a member of the touring party that Rebekah was contractually obliged to get a certain or minimum number of photographs from a celebrity/public relations perspective during the tournament. For example, I recall her setting up photos of her boarding a private plane to Russia. Regarding the World Cup WAG photo I recall being told by a member of the touring party that Rebekah had not asked some of the older ladies present at the hotel to attend the dinner she had arranged. Other ladies featured in the photograph also expressed annoyance and dissatisfaction to me at being set up to be in the photograph orchestrated by Rebekah. One of the players in the squad told me directly that he was also angry at this set-up as they did not court public attention with their private lives. Similarly, Harry Maguire's then girlfriend, Fern [Hawkins], later expressed her upset to me that she had taken part and commented that she was embarrassed, wasn't prepared and hadn't expected to be put in that position.'

Rebekah Vardy denied in court that she had encouraged the women to pose for a group photo, knowing that a press photographer had been tipped off and was waiting to capture the shot. However, when asked for details by Coleen's barrister, she blamed heavy drinking for failing to remember the details of the paparazzi shot.

The group of WAGs in the snap included Marcus Rashford's girlfriend Lucia Loi, Kyle Walker's partner Annie Kilner and Maguire's fiancée Hawkins. Rebekah said her publicist, Caroline Watt, had arranged for a photographer to take pictures of her as she left her hotel but denied giving the photographer the location of either the hotel or the restaurant where the WAGs were having dinner. The court heard Rebekah texted Watt about travel arrangements from the hotel to the restaurant. There were exchanges about last-minute changes in travel arrangements on the night. The following night, the girls were on the town again for the usual up market meal at Sunday Ginza in Saint Petersburg. Social media posts showed the women laughing as they sipped champagne and tried hookah pipes at the swanky restaurant and bar where Cristal Rose cost 8,353 rubles (£100).

There were further disputes over the seating arrangements in the stadium and Rebekah clashed again with Robertson. The FA officer complained in her statement that Rebekah had labelled her seat allocation for the semi-final against Croatia, which England lost 2-1 in extra time, as 'unacceptable' despite being in a category one area and the best seats being dished out on rotation to 'keep things fair'.

'Becky had a private jet to ferry her around to games so didn't spend as much time with the group of women, but nevertheless they trusted her,' said a source. 'Many of them feel very sad.' Fern Hawkins, who later married England and Manchester United defender Harry Maguire, was particularly upset.

Nicola McClean is married to Tom Williams, who now plays for Hashtag United of the Essex Senior League. Tom is a defender and midfielder who made nearly 300 appearances in the Football League for numerous clubs, including QPR and West Ham. The I'm A Celebrity Get Me Out Of Here star has been married to Tom since 2009, told Closer Magazine in 2020: 'I've had different experiences at different clubs but the WAG world can be a b****y mean girls like existence...There can be rivalry and unfriendliness with someone in the group and the top dog and there can be a lot of drama. It isn't just amazing holidays and designer clothes there can be a lot of behind-the-scenes politics between the girls. A lot of women want to emulate Victoria Beckham; Alex Gerrard, Elen Rivas - they dine out on the fact they're a WAG and it can consume you.' Nicola then pointed out that all is not as it seems with Mrs Vardy and Mrs

Rooney: 'I know some WAGs will only be interested in the hierarchy, fame and drama but I don't believe Rebekah is like that. She's not fussed about the press or limelight. Everyone thinks Coleen is really private - but remember she's done countless interviews, books and even her own TV show.'

We all loved little Leicester pulling off the all time most unlikely 5,000-1 title triumph, yet even that is now tainted by the interfering, publicity seeking, vengeful, and on the make WAGs. We discovered that Danny Drinkwater, with whom Jamie achieved what most people thought to be impossible - winning the Premier League title with Leicester in 2016 - was offered up to the papers following his arrest for drink-driving after crashing his Range Rover in 2019, while information was also leaked to the press on the then Leicester winger Riyad Mahrez because the lads were seething that the Manchester City bound winger couldn't be bothered to turn up for training for a couple of days.

BILLY & JOY

WAGs might seem like a new phenomena but the first WAG of real consequence goes all the way back to the England captain and his girl friend singer. Yes, of course Posh & Becks. Well, no, not quite! In fact the first Golden Couple of English football, the nation's captain and one of the country's top singing stars, goes all the way back to the 1950s.

Billy Wright & Joy Beverley of the Beverley Sisters were one of the most glamorous couples of their generation, long before the term WAG had even been thought of. Their marriage occurred at a time before the era of footballers being known for having celebrity girlfriends. This was in July 1958, by which time Wright was 34, and it proved to be one of the most successful showbiz marriages.

While the Beverley Sisters were adored by the nation, Billy was one of the country's greatest ever captains. Joy was known as 'the middle one' of the Beverley Sisters, who had hits with 'Sisters', 'I Saw Mommy Kissing Santa Claus' and 'Little Drummer Boy'. The singer, from Bethnal Green in London, was the eldest sister in the trio. They had their own BBC TV show in the 1950s and were awarded MBEs in 2006.

Joy, born Joycelyn V Chinery in 1924, and twin sisters Babs and Teddie, born in 1927, were brought up in east London. Their parents were George and Victoria Beverley - who performed as music-hall duo, Coram and Mills. During their formative years money was scarce and the sisters shared a bed until they were teenagers. Speaking in 2002, Joy insisted they did not notice being poor. "Mother was very clever," she told the Independent. "If we said we wanted a bike, she'd say: 'Oh, I love you too much to give you a bike.'"

During the Second World War the girls were evacuated to the Midlands. There they secured a contract to become "Bonnie Babies" in an advertising campaign for the bedtime drink Ovaltine. Radio appearances for the BBC followed and with support from bandleader Glenn Miller they became professional singers, renowned for their close harmonies and glamorous lifestyles. After the war the siblings were given their own TV show, initially called Three Little Girls in View and later retitled Those Beverley Sisters as the group's profile improved. In 1951 the trio signed a recording contract with Columbia Records that helped them become the highest paid female act in the UK, earning more than £700 a week at a time when the average weekly wage was £5. They were the first British female group to break into the US top 10 and enjoyed chart success with Christmas records such as 'I Saw Mommy Kissing Santa Claus'. Other favourites included 'Bye Bye Love' and 'Always and Forever'.

But they all but retired after Joy married Billy. "I felt it was time we had an ordinary life," she recalled in a 1995 interview. "We'd had a successful career and I felt no guilt." But the trio reunited in the 1980s, resurrecting old songs such as 'It's Illegal, It's Immoral Or It Makes You Fat' for gay clubs and variety shows. The sisters entered the Guinness Book Of Records in 2002, as the world's longest surviving vocal group without a change in the line up. That same year they sang for the Queen and Duke of Edinburgh at a Jubilee concert. In 2006, the group were awarded MBEs for services to music, and arrived at Buckingham Palace - as always - in identical outfits.

Apart from their hugely successful careers, they were far removed from the modern day

WAG and their glitzy husbands. Of course there were no multi-million pound football contracts back then, so Billy and Joy lived fairly ordinary lives for such big celebrities, had a large family, had no vices, unsavoury episodes and didn't have an army of social media gurus or PR people in tow.

Wright hit the big time as a player when he converted to centre half and spent his entire club career at Wolverhampton Wanderers where he made 541 first-team appearances for the club where there is a statue in his honour outside Molineux. In 1993, when Wolves redeveloped the Molineux Stadium, the main stand was named the Billy Wright Stand. The club commissioned a 15ft high bronze statue of Billy that was erected three years later, outside the stand, in front of the club's main entrance. Sadly, Billy never lived to see this wonderful tribute to him. He died of pancreatic cancer in 1994 at the age of 70 and Wolverhampton came to a standstill for his funeral as fans paid their respects in the pouring rain. He was cremated and his ashes were scattered on the pitch at Molineux.

He led his country with distinction and great dignity. Billy became the first footballer in the world to earn 100 international caps, Wright still holds the record for the longest unbroken run in competitive international football. He made a total of 105 appearances for England, captaining them a record 90 times, including during the

1950, 1954 and 1958 World Cup finals.

His 70 successive appearances for his country was a record later equalled by Bobby Moore. He led Wolves to victory in the 1949 FA Cup final and to three First Division championship titles before retiring in 1959 when he was made a CBE and life member of the FA.

He became manager of England's youth team in 1960, before being appointed manager of Arsenal in 1962, replacing George Swindin. Arsenal started strongly under Wright, finishing seventh in 1962-63, qualifying for Europe for the first time in their history. Wright signed Bob Wilson, Joe Baker, Frank McLintock and Ian Ure who would go on to win honours for the Gunners but Wright won only 38.46% of his matches in charge, the lowest rate for any post-war Arsenal manager (caretaker managers excepted). After a poor 1965-66 season – where Arsenal finished 14th and were knocked out of the FA Cup by Blackburn Rovers (who finished bottom of the First Division) — Wright was dismissed by the Arsenal board in the summer of 1966.

After leaving Arsenal, Wright successfully overcame alcoholism and later became a television pundit and Head of Sport for ATV and Central Television, before retiring in 1989. The following year he joined the board of directors at Wolves as part of the takeover by Sir Jack Hayward. On 7 August 1993, he presented

Manchester United with the FA Charity Shield, which they won on penalties against Arsenal at Wembley. On 7 December that year he was present for a friendly game against Honved of Hungary which commemorated the re-opening of Molineux as a rebuilt 28,525-seat stadium. The redevelopment saw three new stands built at the stadium in the space of two years, with the one replacing the Waterloo Road Stand being designated the Billy Wright Stand.

He was the subject of This Is Your Life on two occasions: in May 1961 when he was surprised by Eamonn Andrews at the EMI Studios in London's St John's Wood, and in January 1990, when Michael Aspel surprised him at Thames Television's Teddington Studios. He was appointed a Commander of the Order of the British Empire on 13 June 1959.[9]

Billy and London-born Joy married on July 28, 1958 at Poole Register Office. They were married for 36 years until Billy's death from cancer in September 1994. Joy lived until 91, passing away in 2015 when then Wolves vice-president Baroness Rachael Heyhoe-Flint commented: "During Billy's time at the club from when Sir Jack took over in 1990 she became very much associated with Wolves and I vividly remember Joy and the other Beverley Sisters leading us in song at the opening of the Billy Wright stand in 1993."

Joy and Billy had three children - Vince,

Vicky and Babette, and three granddaughters and one grandson. I got to know Vince when we were fledgling journalists at rival local papers, and later knew Billy when he was a TV executive. But few knew Billy and his life more intimately than his biographer and prolific author Norman Giller. I asked Norman for an insight into Bill and he told me: "Billy and Joy were Posh and Becks in black and white. He was the 34-year-old captain of England and League champions Wolves when they met, and the Beverley Sisters were, relatively speaking, the most famous close harmony group of that 1950s era, the Spice Girls of their time. After a whirlwind courtship they got married in what was supposed to be secret in 1958, but the news was leaked and Poole was brought to a standstill with thousands of people blocking the streets around Poole registry office. The Sisters (Joy and twins Teddie and Babs) were topping the bill at Bournemouth Hippodrome at the time. Billy was coming to the end of a career in which he was the first player in the world to win 100 caps, and the photographers had a ball capturing the Sisters at Wembley watching him lead out England for his 100th match against Scotland."

Again Norman, who has recently written a best selling biography of Jimmy Greaves, is best suited to analyse the lifestyles of the first celebrity couple and the current day WAGs. He tells me: "The contrast with today's WAGs could not have been greater. Billy was on the maximum £20-a-week and living modestly in digs in Wolverhampton. The vivacious Joy was a much bigger earner and hooked the man considered one of Britain's most eligible bachelors. They did their 'courting' out of the spotlight and rarely got into the gossip columns until one of the tabloids dragged up a story about Joy's brief first marriage to an America musician. It was splashed on the front page during England's challenge for the World Cup in Sweden in the summer of 1958. Billy, the most mild mannered of men, blew his top when he got an after-midnight call from a headline seeking reporter. That was when he and Joy hatched their plan to get married in secret.

"Stan Cullis, Billy's stern and serious manager at Wolves, would not have allowed a woman anywhere near the training ground or the dressing-room on match days. He would have been frothing at the mouth over the Rooney/Vardy battle and would have knocked their heads together long before their feud got to court.

"It's worth noting that at his playing peak David Beckham earned more in a week than Billy picked up throughout his playing career. For most of it he was on £11 and then £17-a-week. He spent 21 years with Wolves and his England career spanned 13 years. If Becks had been time machined back to Billy's era he would have thought he had landed on another planet. And

'WAGs' back then meant witty people or excited dogs!"

When Billy took off his England shirt with the Three Lions, I fully expected to see three lions tattooed on his heart.

BOBBY ROBSON

Billy's love for the game was always something that we shared. He was a great player, an amazing captain and I felt really honoured to follow in his footsteps in earning 100 caps for my country.

DAVID BECKHAM

I feel proud and humbled to be following in the footsteps of the great Billy Wright in captaining Wolverhampton Wanderers . His presence can be felt the minute you walk through the doors at Molineux.

CONOR COADY

TINA AND BOBBY

Tina and Bobby Moore were the Golden Couple of their generation, back when the national team actually won something! Blond and good looking, Bobby and Tina were a star couple in their day; Bobby, the suave national hero who wiped his hands before shaking the Queen by the hand and lifting the World Cup and his gorgeous wife Tina was the undisputed Queen of what we know as the WAGs. Such was the power of their love story that it was brought to life in the 2017 ITV mini series *Tina and Bobby*, with Coronation Street star Michelle Keegan playing the blonde bombshell WAG. Their story had a bit everything: the glamour and danger of the East End in the sixties when the notorious Kray twins ruled the roost, World Cup glory, Bobby's regular night out with close friends such as Jimmy Greaves and of course his arrest in Colombia on suspicion of theft before the 1970 World Cup.

Tina and Bobby had met in the at the Ilford Palais nightclub in Essex in 1957 when she was just 15 and he was 16 - and for both of them it was love at first sight. It mirrors the first love of Coleen and Wayne. After five years of romance they married in 1962 but just two years after their marriage, the couple were struck by heart-

breaking news when Bobby was diagnosed with testicular cancer at just 23. Tina was pregnant with their first child, Roberta, when she was given the devastating diagnosis. She told *The Sun*: "It was up to the next of kin to decide whether a patient was told they had cancer. It was a death sentence in those days. I pleaded with the surgeon not to tell him. I was very worried for the baby and for Bobby. I didn't know if he was going to live or die."

Bobby had one of his testicles removed and 14 months later, following an amazing recovery, he lead his country to World Cup glory. Overnight, everything changed for the young, glamorous couple with Tina propelled into the world of showbiz. On the night of England's stunning victory, Bobby and Tina celebrated at the Playboy club and they counted film stars and musical legends among their closest friends. Sean Connery and his wife were so fond of the couple they even once babysat for them while they were in Spain. Tina tried her hand at modelling and starred in a Bisto advert and it seemed nothing could go wrong for the happy couple. But in 1970, Tina and the couple's children, Roberta and Dean, were at the heart of a terrifying kidnap plot and there were threats to shoot Bobby during a West Ham game. Bobby retired in 1978 and, having missed out on the Watford manager's job he was besieged with money problems, which Tina believed led to depression. Bobby took a job managing a football club in Hong Kong but when he returned in 1982, the couple's financial situation had become perilous. She believed the pressure caused Bobby to find solace in the arms of another woman - something Tina was not prepared to put up with. Tina insisted her husband was not a womaniser but when she gave him an ultimatum, he left - and she was heartbroken. The couple divorced in 1986 and Bobby went on to marry Stephanie Parlane in 1991, two years before his death from bowel and liver cancer aged just 51. Tina, desperate to escape being seen as Bobby's first wife, moved to America. Tragically, their son, Dean, died at just 43 in 2011.

Rebekah Vardy spent £140,000 on travel to Russia for the World Cup in a private jet, back in 1966 three of the wives took the train to London where England played all their matches. Patricia Hunt, who was then married to Liverpool and England forward Roger, recalls: 'I met up with Pat Wilson [wife of defender Ray] and Norma Charlton [married to Bobby] at Warrington and we all went down together on the train to Wembley. We were completely anonymous, of course. No one made a fuss or noticed us. It's not like it is today. As far as the players were concerned, we didn't come anywhere near them. The attitude was that they are there to do their job, and when that's over you can see them. We watched the match and then came back home again. We didn't even see the husbands. It was just very ordinary in a way.'

Rebekah has spoken openly about the sex lives of today's players and admitted that she and her husband 'struggle' to be intimate during the tournament: 'There is no sex ban, but I think we'd struggle to do it anyway with the kids around — it wouldn't work logistically!' By contrast Mrs Hunt, while not mentioning Vardy by name says she's not a fan of the more lairy type of modern footballer's wife. Speaking of the 2018 WAGs, she said, 'You have to have your boobs done and false hair and false teeth and false nails. They're not real, are they? The way that the WAGs are seems to be based on how people on reality TV look. They seem to copy that look and not want to be your ordinary grassroots people. Well, I don't know how you come home from all that flash and live an ordinary life.'

Yet while they may have been happy to stay in the background during the tournament, the Wives of '66 rebelled when they were separated from their partners after the final. The Football Association excluded them from the champagne reception at London's Royal Garden Hotel in Kensington, instead, the wives — and one fiancée — dined separately in the chop house upstairs. Their husbands came up to collect them at around midnight.

Kathleen Peters, the wife of midfielder Martin Peters, said: 'We were overwhelmed and just sat in the hotel room, staring at his medal like two kids. We didn't even drink champagne — I think I made us a cup of tea.' One wife was absent; Jack Charlton's wife Pat, who — now 83 — likes to joke that she is the 'oldest WAG in the world'. She watched the World Cup Final on a black-and-white TV in her modest semi-detached house in Leeds with her mother. 'Of course we were very proud of them, but we were not involved like the wives and girlfriends are these days at all,' she says. Pat was pregnant and opted to stay at home for medical reasons. 'I watched it at home because I was about to have a baby. I already had two children. I wanted to go to the final, but the medical advice was against it and you don't want to go into labour in the middle of the World Cup Final at Wembley.

'I know that some of the girls were upset because after the final they could not sit with the husbands but had to go into another room for dinner. They felt it was not right, stuck in a different room, like you are nothing. But that was the way it was.' Pat, married to Jack for 60 plus years, remembers he rang her about an hour after the match, and came home the next day — stopping at a transport cafe for a plate of egg and chips. Separations while the tournament was on were hard, she said. 'They would go off for two or three weeks before the World Cup and you wouldn't see them.' That was England manager Alf Ramsey's way and no one dare cross him. He didn't want his players to have any contact with their wives — they were allowed phone calls and letters.

Patricia Hunt, who divorced from Roger in 1981, explains: 'We had a very different relationship with the management. They kept the wives and families at a distance. We were definitely not involved or invited. Our role was not even considered.' She was shocked that Fabian Delph was allowed to return from Russia to the UK to be with his wife for the birth of their third child. 'If that had happened in Alf Ramsey's day, he would have said: "Go home...and don't come back after." It would not even have been considered a possibility. Football is not just a game any more. The money they earn, the cars they drive, the mansions they live in and the lifestyles they lead are totally different from the way it was for us.'

Bobby Moore, Geoff Hurst and Martin Peters formed the backbone of Sir Alf's team educated in the traditional, ball retaining way by Ron Greenwood at West Ham. In those days the managers negotiated the transfers and sorted out the players wages. Martin Peters later earned around £120 a week at Tottenham (the equivalent of £1,770). Harry Kane earns £200,000 a week. Pat Hunt says: 'We were ordinary people. Your husband was playing a game of football, but it no big fuss made. I would have hated to have been looked at and analysed and watched as the WAGs are, but now it's all big money and celebrity.

'Rebekah Vardy flies out with all the family on a private jet, then she's on the telly on Loose Women and is out until 3am or 4am, and it's all about publicity. I suppose they do it and absolutely love it, and good luck to them, if they can handle it.'

Tina Moore agreed. 'We didn't have anything like their money, but what we did have was a wonderful life. Would I like to be a WAG today? I don't know, to be honest. My husband was handsome and charismatic, but you never had too much concern (about predatory female rivals). Nowadays its horrendous — women pursue footballers because they know that they could end up with a great lifestyle. I wish them luck with it.'

POSH & BECKS

The haircuts, the free-kicks, the tabloid scandals, the injury crises, the fashion icon, the pin-up, the fall-outs, David Beckham was at the centre of it all, but none more so than when he married Victoria Adams, nicknamed 'Posh Spice' in girl group the Spice Girls.

Richard Desmond paid out a small fortune back then, £1million, for exclusive rights to the wedding for his celebrity magazine offshoot of his blossoming media empire, *OK! Magazine*. Editor Martin Townsend had the task of capturing every moment and capturing images from the day that helped that edition sell over one million copies - a triumph for the magazine, the publisher who took a huge gamble paying such a large sum and most of all a triumph for , in taking such a huge financial gamble, but most of all it established Posh and Becks as the celebrity couple of their time.

Martin later moved on to edit *the Sunday Express,* and recently took up a PR role as senior Advisor with Pagefield. He tells me: "I don't remember ever speaking to David or Victoria about WAG culture, and it was never something they mentioned. They had quite a selective and long-standing circle of friends and have always been very close-knit with their families, so wouldn't have suddenly started 'hanging out' with people for the sake of a few column inches. I think Victoria and David were probably the model for a lot of WAG couples, who were trying to emulate them and jump on the fame bandwagon, but they are always ahead of trends so I suspect that as soon as WAG culture became a media phenomenon they'd have moved on.

"The essential advantage that Posh & Becks had was that they had separate, highly-successful careers and were each respected in their own right. They didn't have anything to prove. They were - and are - a smart, motivated couple whose ambitions also went far beyond trying to get column inches: David wanted to help youngsters improve their football skills and to be an ambassador for the game, and Victoria was always set on a career in fashion design. They were consummate professionals in their own right and didn't have to move with a pack.

"I met and interviewed them at Victoria's family home in Hertfordshire and at their apartment in Alderley Edge, where David cooked me pasta, and at 'Beckingham Palace' [real name 'Rowneybury House', a mansion set in 24 acres of grounds where the couple lived for 15 years]. They were always very welcoming and friendly."

Much of the Posh & Becks empire was fashioned by the expertise of entertainment publicist Alan Edwards, who was delighted that his clients were not shy about living up to their new billing. As well as knowing Alan intimately and gaining much of verification for stories that came my way as Daily Mirror chief football writer, Martin Townsend became one of my best mates when I moved over to the Express group having been headed-hunted by him on behalf of his proprietor Richard Desmond.

For an insight into the real Posh & Becks, I spoke with my old mate Alan Edwards who has all the credentials for knowing what makes celebrities tick as he told me: 'I started out as PR for the Spice Girls, then became David's PR as well. Later on I became Victor's manager so I was working closely with them both. I also handled for publicity for the Spice Girls come back too. After a stint in music journalism I started working for a PR called Keith Altham in 1975 on bands like The Who and Marc Bolan before setting up my own business and going on to represent Bowie for nearly 40 years, Prince, P. Diddy, Naomi Campbell and Bon Jovi amongst others."

So what makes Posh & Becks tick? Alan says: "All that Posh and Becks thing seems like a distant memory now to be honest. What would I say, they were a class act, media savvy, hard working, fun and a pleasure to work for. "

I would also count on Glenn Hoddle as a personal friend while Becks himself invited me to the launch of his autobiography out in Madrid, sharing a journey back with Garth Crooks after the event, while Becks also signed one of his No 7 long sleeved England shirts to me which I have proudly framed and have hanging on my wall of memorabilia alongside the likes of Pele, Ruud Gullit, Franco Zola, Ossie & Ricky and many others. So, I can look objectively at Beck's career on the front pages as well as the back having heard so many inside stories from both sides.

But as pictures of the Golden Couple leaving restaurants were regularly splashed on the front pages, they were appointed king and queen of British celebrity. 'When I look back at it, I think either "What was I thinking?" or that people must have thought I was flash,' Beckham, who used his United first pay cheque to buy a Tag Heuer watch, told *GQ* in 2016. 'There were certain parts of my childhood or growing up in Manchester as a young professional, where I look back and think people must have thought I was being really flash, but I wasn't.'

Becks got engaged to Victoria in January 1998, five months before his first tournament with England, the 1998 World Cup in France under England manager Glenn Hoddle. Hoddle was one of the brightest young coaching minds to emerge in English football since Ron Greenwood and Sir Alf but that summer would test Glenn in ways he probably hadn't anticipated.

Going into the tournament Becks was the

poster boy for the new England team and he relished working with Hoddle, a player he had idolised growing up in east London. While there was vast experience with the likes of David Seaman, Tony Adams, Paul Ince and captain Alan Shearer, who had all starred for their country in Euro '96, Becks was the new hope alongside a clutch of Manchester United stars who had matured under Sir Alex Ferguson and helped turn the club into a dominant force in domestic football. So there was quite a lot of expectation heaped on the shoulders of 23-year-old Beckham which only grew following the omission of the previous star man, Paul Gascoigne.

Hoddle had shown by the way he ditched Gazza from his World Cup squad in La Manga, the thrashing of the hotel room, and the players relationship with Sheryl, that the new England manager had only one thing on his mind - he wanted a team capable of winning the World Cup in a country where he had learned so much under Arsene Wenger at Monaco and no distractions among his players.

Becks had won only 15 caps by June 1998, but was firmly established as a starter in Hoddle's team, having been the only player to feature in every qualifying match under him. Ahead of the tournament, his sponsor Adidas projected his face onto the White Cliffs of Dover, alongside the tagline "England Expects". The magnitude of this new found fame hit Beckham shortly before that World Cu. He told *FourFourTwo* magazine, 'The other day I was round at Victoria's house and the postman rang the bell to deliver something. I answered the door and his jaw dropped. He said, "Blimey, I never thought I'd see a legend this early in the morning". That's just daft – I'm no legend. I can't believe this is all happening to me.'

Ahead of England's opening game against Tunisia in Marseille on June 15, Beckham attracted attention by hanging out with Elton John at his house on the French Riviera a week before the tournament, where he was photographed wearing a Jean-Paul Gaultier sarong, rather than attend an 'optional' golf day with the England squad.

'Sarongs are great,' Beckham he explained on the ITV morning show *Lorraine* in 2014. 'That's one thing I never regret because I thought it looked great and I would still wear it now.'

Hoddle felt Beckham had become distracted with his celebrity life style. He had always intended to make Becks central to his team, but held him back for the first two games as Hoddle's side beat Tunisia 2-0 and before a shock 2-1 defeat to Romania. 'Fine, he's in love,' Hoddle noted in his World Cup diary, failing to disguise the inference, 'but I think he lost his way a bit at the end of last season and his form suffered as a result.'

In his recent autobiography *Playmaker: My Life and the Love of Football*, Hoddle revealed: 'Going into our opening game against Tunisia, however, I could tell that David wasn't focused enough in training. My decision to replace him with Darren Anderton caused a fuss but it was the right call. David would have played at right wing-back if his mind was clear but he was distracted by events off the pitch. I was honest with David when I sat down with him. "I don't think you're focused," I said. "I'm going to leave you out of this game. Your mind is somewhere else. I don't know what it is, but you've got to get your mind right." I looked him in the eye and made sure to give him some encouragement. "You will play at this World Cup," I added. "You're too good to leave out but I need you right at it." It jolted David. He wasn't happy but his response was excellent. He was on it when we trained the next day. He hit a new level and showed me that it wouldn't be a risk to play him in midfield with 'Incey' [Paul Ince] further down the line. The matter was over as far as I was concerned. But the press had other ideas. David was a huge name and his omission was a big story.'

Sir Alex Ferguson criticised Hoddle's management in his *Sunday Times* column after Beckham was sent to face the press despite being dropped. Hoddle felt that was a bit rich as Fergie had also detected issues surrounding his player's private life, but as usual was determined to be perverse, with the right intentions for his club, to back his own player.

Hoddle says in his autobiography: 'It certainly didn't go down well with Alex Ferguson – and I wasn't exactly flavour of the month at Old Trafford. I had left out Phil Neville and had issues with another United player when I had to discipline Teddy Sheringham after he was pictured on a night out in the build-up to the tournament. Dealing with United wasn't easy. There were problems getting players to report for duty at times and I had a row with Ferguson over two of his players before one friendly. His conduct was unprofessional when we spoke on the phone. I wasn't going to use the players but I wanted them to join up because we were preparing for the World Cup. But he wasn't having it. He was ranting and raving, even when I said I would send them back once the meetings were out of the way. I can't repeat what he called me. I just put the phone down. He called back to apologise but he wasn't happy. It all became a bit of a battle, and he used his Sunday Times column to criticise me when David and Gary Neville were put up at a press conference shortly after our win over Tunisia. Apparently it was insensitive after they'd been left out of the game. There was no big strategy on my part. I wasn't trying to humiliate David. It was down to the press officers to select players and I gave the thumbs up when they suggested David. I knew the media wanted to speak to him and I thought it was a good idea to give them what they wanted on a quiet day, especially as David was guaranteed to play sooner rather than later.'

Becks returned to the starting line-up in the final group game, scoring a trademark free-kick in a 2-0 win over Colombia which ensured England advanced to the knockout stage where they would face Argentina, rather than Croatia, after finishing second in Group G. It was 12 years after Diego Maradona's Hand of God goal and 16 years after the Falklands War, but no one had forgiven or forgotten in Argentina. 'After tonight, England vs Argentina will be remembered for what a player did with his feet,' Adidas' pre-match promotion, which featured Beckham, provocatively proclaimed. Beckham was selected in central midfield alongside Ince and Paul Scholes, with Hoddle playing an attack-minded 3-5-2 formation against Argentina, who had beaten Japan, Jamaica and Croatia in the group stage without conceding a goal. It was an instant classic; 18 year-old Michael Owen, who had come off the bench and scored an equaliser against Romania, tore Argentina apart. Diego Simeone won an early penalty when David Seaman brought him down, Gabriel Batistuta converting from the spot before Owen was clipped in the box and Alan Shearer also made no mistake from 12 yards:1-1. Then Beckham picked out Owen who outpaced the Argentina defence and smashing the ball home - England were 2-1 up after just 16 minutes. However despite dominating the game England went in at the break with the scores level, after Javier Zanetti's levelled on the stroke of half-time. Then came that fateful moment, in which it all changed for Beckham and England.

Two minutes into the second half Diego Simeone came flying through the back of Beckham, as he got up he whispered a few words into Beckham's ear and Becks kicked out at Simeone's calf right under the referee's nose. Down he went. Kim Milton Nielsen brandished the red card. 'Let's just say the referee fell into the trap,' was Simeone's assessment years later. 'You could say that my falling transformed a yellow card into a red card. In fact, the most appropriate punishment was a yellow. Obviously, I was being clever.'

England went on to have a late goal in extra-time baffling ruled out and lost on penalty kicks once more. Afterwards Hoddle offered a half-hearted defence of his player. 'David Beckham's sending off cost us dearly. I am not denying it cost us the game. But it would be wrong to put the blame on David Beckham's shoulders or anybody's shoulders. I'm not looking for someone to blame. I just hope that the country next year respect the fact that he has done fantastic in the past. And he has got a great, great future - we would be cutting our noses off to spite our face.'

'This is without doubt the worst moment of my career,' Beckham admitted, 'I will always regret my actions during last night's game. I have apologised to the England players and management and I want every England supporter to know how deeply sorry I am.'

The headlines the next day were not kind: 'TEN HEROIC LIONS, ONE STUPID BOY' sniped the Daily Mirror. 'MOMENT OF LUNACY THAT COST CUP HOPES' added the more fatherly Daily Mail. Two days later the Mirror had Beckham's face at the middle of a dart board: 'Still Bitter? Take your fury out on our David Beckham dartboard' which invited readers to 'hurl away' at Beckham, who they say 'earns £8 million a year, dates Posh Spice, wears sarongs and dyes his hair.' Beckham was the bullseye of a board that also featured Argentina's leader during the Falklands War, Leopoldo Galtieri, referee Nielsen and presenter Jeremy Beadle. The Telegraph branded him a 'Gaultier-saronged, Posh Spiced, Cooled Britannia, look-at-me, what-a-lad, loadsamoney, sex-and-shopping, fame-schooled, daytime-TV, over-coiffed twerp'.

When Beckham returned he was chased through Heathrow Airport by a hoard of baying journalists with one shouting 'How does it feel to let your country down?' adding 'Do you realise what you've done?'. He escaped to the soccer wasteland of New York where he took refuge with Victoria on a Spice Girls tour.

During the tournament the Pleasant Pheasant pub in South Norwood had a Beckham mascot for the tournament - a life-size dummy dressed in a sarong and an England shirt with 'Beckham 7' on the back. Now, it was suspended from scaffolding as an effigy.

Beckham later accused Hoddle of 'feeding the frenzy' as he received death threats and bullets in the post, while a man stood menacingly outside his house in the middle of the night, disappearing before the police arrived.

'I made a mistake in '98 and the reaction at the time was pretty brutal,' Beckham said as part of a Heads Up campaign, 'if social media was around when I was going through that time, it would have been a whole different story, but I was lucky, I had a support system within Manchester United, the manager, and obviously family.' 'He could hardly have been more vilified if he'd committed murder or high treason,' his manager Ferguson later said, while England and United team-mate Gary Neville criticised the FA for 'rubber-dinghy management: they chuck you overboard and look after their own'.

Somehow Becks comeback from all of that, a testimony to his determination to be the best in his sport, and his mental approach changed overnight. Within twelve months he had landed an unsurpassed treble of Premier League, FA Cup and European Cup with Manchester United and as his club dominated the European club football more trophies and accolades came his way - he played in three more World Cups, and would have become only the second England player to be involved in four (after Bobby Charlton) if injury hadn't ruled him out of Fabio Capello's squad for South Africa. He also moved to Real Madrid in 2003 to become one of the clubs 'galacticos' wowing crowds in Spain with his technical ability, a first for Englishman playing there.

Hoddle, though, has no regrets in leaving out his young hopeful from the start of the World Cup in France. 'It makes me laugh when I hear that I was jealous of David Beckham's fame. This is a player I wanted to sign on loan at Chelsea. I gave him his England debut. David's technique was incredible and I've never seen anyone cross the ball as well as him. His passing range was impeccable and I think that he could have played more in central midfield for club and country when he was older.'

The WAGs were most prominent in the Germany World Cup of 2006. Based in Baden Baden they stole the show with their showbiz glamour and tabloid reporters competed for shots of the player's wives and girlfriends wearing tight-fitting vest tops, short shorts and questionable knee-high boots. England didn't win, of course, but their WAGs were a No 1 hit and suddenly people without much interest in the sport took notice of the extraordinary multi million pounds lives of the footballer's partners. There was far more interest in the WAGs squad than the one trying their best, and failing yet again, in a World Cup tournament. The original super squad included Victoria, Coleen Rooney, Cheryl Cole, Ellen Rivas, Abbey Clancy, Louise Owen and Carly Zucker. The Victoria half of brand Becks was the original Queen WAG in 2006. At the time Victoria had been married to David for seven years and had just given birth to her third boy, Cruz. She had just launched her denim line, DVB Style and took to the catwalk for Roberto Cavalli. Coleen Rooney had risen to fame as a WAG at just 20 years old. However Wayne's repeated cheating strained the relationship over the years. Lingerie model Abbey was a finalists in Britain's Next Top Model and began dating Peter Crouch that same year. Carly Zucker was by then known as Carly Cole after marrying midfielder Joe Cole in Chelsea in 2009, Carly loved to party during the 2006 World Cup. Former nail technician Alex Curran began dating Steven Gerrard in 2002, but she became one of the leading figures in the 2006 WAG squad; the couple married in 2007. Fashion lover Alex has released a perfume, fronted a Lipsy campaign and has written a weekly shopping column for a national newspaper. Despite being married to one of the most famous footballers at the time, Louise Owen wasn't your stereotype

WAG as she always managed to keep her distance from the limelight.

Elen Rivas was engaged to Frank Lampard at the time of the World Cup, and therefore became a permanent fixture in the WAG circle. After splitting from Frank after a seven-year relationship, she dated Peter Andre, appeared on Dancing On Ice and now looks after her two daughters Luna and Isla while working as a model. Frank has since married TV presenter Christine Bleakley.

That was not the only star studded celebrity double act to find love faded fast. Back then, 23-year-old Cheryl was a star in Girls Aloud and had just married Ashley Cole. Not long into her rise to fame, Cheryl started dating Ashley. Cheryl and Ashley met after living in the same complex when Cheryl first found fame with Girls Aloud. The pair exchanged numbers in their shared car park and embarked on a number of "secret" dates. The loved-up pair got married in 2006, penning a six-figure magazine deal at the time. Ashley was one of the best ever left backs to play in the Premier League. Born in Stepney, London, Cole began his youth career at Arsenal and made his full debut for the club in November 1999, making 228 appearances, scoring nine times for the North London club. With Arsenal he won two Premier League titles, three FA Cups, and was an integral member of the "Invincibles" team of the 2003–04 season, who went the entire league season undefeated. Cole made an appearance in Arsenal's first Champions League final in 2006; the club lost 2–1 to Barcelona. However, it started to turn sour for the 'golden couple' when Ashley was accused of 'cheating' on Cheryl just months after their wedding. Despite forgiving him, Ashley continued with his wandering ways, with allegations that he'd been unfaithful rocking their romance yet again. It got too much for 'Chez' in 2010, when she filed for divorce. Ashley's former Arsenal teammate Jermaine Pennant made the shocking claim that Ashley had cheated on Cheryl with five women in his new autobiography Mental: Bad Behaviour, Ugly Truths and the Beautiful Game.

But the 2006 World cup is remembered more for the exploits of the WAGs off the field then their hubbies on it. At the time The X Factor and Big Brother were still on Channel 4. Girls Aloud scored two number 1 singles with 'Sound of the Underground' and 'I'll Stand By You' and had two sell out tours. Coleen was still Coleen McLaughlin in 2006 but due to her relationship with Wayne, she was already well known before the World Cup, thanks to her best-selling workout DVD and ITV programme *Coleen's Real Women*. After the tournament, she penned an autobiography - *Welcome to My World* - in 2007, released her own perfume and landed a £3m campaign with George at Asda. Coleen married Wayne in a luxurious wedding in Portofino in 2008 and sold rights to *OK magazine*, for £2.5million.

The Three Lions, under the leadership of Sven Goran Eriksson, had headed to Germany for the 2006 tournament full of the usual hope and bravado after winning their group, with two wins and a draw. Unfortunately football failed to come home yet again, instead football brought their homes with them. England crashed out yet again on penalties, this time to Portugal in the quarter finals but the WAGs, whether in the stands or out on the town in Baden-Baden, attracted most of the attention and were the World Cup's No 1 glamour 'team'. They were also No 1 for racking up huge bar and hotel bills, singing and dancing on tables and there was even a drug scandal. Abbey's World Cup was brought to an abrupt end after pictures surfaced in the press of her taking cocaine. Although the photos were from a few years earlier, her then boyfriend, Peter Crouch ended their relationship - soon after the tournament , saying: 'I wish to make the situation absolutely clear: Abbey and I were in the very early stages of a relationship which, for a number of reasons, I decided a few weeks ago to end, and I accordingly informed Abi of my decision.' That same summer, Abbey appeared on *Britain's Next Top Model*, finishing second and later going on to host the show nearly a decade later. She and Peter eventually reunited and married in Sardinia in 2009. They now have four children, two daughters and two sons. Abbey has been on TV regularly since 2006, as well as *BNTM*, she was a contestant on *Hell's Kitchen* and *Strictly Come Dancing*, which she won at the end of 2013.

Elen Rivas was captured standing on a table belting out 'I Will Survive' in a German bar. Elen and Frank had a daughter before the World Cup and went onto have another before they split in 2009. Speaking after their split, she said: 'Going out with a footballer means you sometimes lose your own identity. It becomes all about them and no one else. But now my life is far more balanced. It is about me and my girls. And that's how it will remain.' Elen appeared on Dancing on Ice in 2011.

The outlandish party girls of 2006 was the reason behind partners being completely banned from the next World Cup in South Africa. Alex Curran had been in Germany to cheer on her boyfriend, Liverpool star Steven Gerrard. She was the WAG famous for running up the colossal hotel bill of £25,000, which included 60 bottles of pink champagne. Alex and Steven got married in Buckinghamshire in 2007 and have four children. Former WAG Lizzie Cundy told *Closer*, 'There wasn't one newspaper or magazine where they weren't on the front cover. They looked so glitzy, and people were desperate to read about them.'

The glitz and glamour didn't stop with the

players, England boss Sven-Goran Eriksson loved a touch of glamour himself, and ended up embroiled in his own kiss and tell tabloid stories, yet he defended his decision to allow the WAGs to stay in the same German spa town as the squad dismissing the allegation that their presence became a distraction as 'a stupid excuse'.

Rio Ferdinand described the paparazzi frenzy that engulfed Baden-Baden as 'like a circus', adding that 'football became a secondary element' so Fabio Capello decided WAGs would only be allowed to meet their partners after each game in South Africa in 2010. Asked if Capello's stance proved he was more of a disciplinarian as England coach, Eriksson said, 'I don't know. Is that to be tough or not tough, inviting the wives and girlfriends? Yes or no? [Their presence] shouldn't have made an impact. England in the past, I can't speak about now, are not different from any other country in the world. The Swedes do the same as we did [in 2006]. The Germans, too. Everyone.'

Eriksson was asked if the players had used the WAGs as an excuse. 'It's a stupid excuse, isn't it? The WAGs were invited when I thought it was the right occasion to do it, and that didn't happen very often. So that's not an excuse. It had absolutely nothing to do with the football. I didn't read the papers or listen to the radio once we'd been eliminated, but I guess people were saying that everything had been wrong. It's always like that, isn't it? The delusion. Huge. Everything was wrong, I suppose, and nothing was right. But that is the way it is. The expectation is always there with England. You know that it is almost as if England must already have won the World Cup even before a ball has been kicked in the finals. I guess you can't do anything about that. It's a danger when expectations go through the roof, but that's the beauty of it as well.'

Yet Sven was seen as culpable in England's failure because he had his own WAG to keep him company on lonely nights, and during the day Nancy Dell'Olio was out on the town with the other WAGs. The Germans found it amusing to say the least as the WAGs stormed the luxury boutiques of Baden-Baden, spending 80,000 euros in one hour, according to a report in the mass-market daily *Bild* which named the six out on the spending spree as Victoria, Coleen, Melanie Slade (girlfriend of Theo Walcott), Cheryl Tweedy (Ashley Cole) and Nancy Dell'Olio (coach Sven-Goran Eriksson) had gone on a manic shopping spree. 'While their bread-winners trained for the next match on Tuesday, the ladies worked on their shopping endurance,' *Bild* said. The women spent 4,395 euros in 10 minutes alone on shoes and T-shirts, with the rest going for creations from Dolce and Gabbana, Prada and Versace, according to the report. 'I hope England stays in the competition for a while,' commented delighted boutique owner Monika Scholz.

After enjoying a scandal-free World Cup in 2006 pregnant with Wayne Bridge's baby, Vanessa Perroncel found herself at the centre of a WAG drama three years later when she was accused of having an affair with Bridge's Chelsea and England teammate John Terry. Wayne turned his back on an international career as a result and refused to shake John's hand on the pitch before a game. After their relationship ended, Vanessa was linked to Cheryl Cole's ex Jean Bernard, while Wayne is now happily married to Saturdays singer turned Loose Women star Frankie Sandford, with whom he has had two children.

Today's more up market, hugely wealthy WAGs aren't too keen on the label they've inherited. Frankie she finds the term 'frustrating', adding 'It used to annoy me because I'd think I've worked for years in the public eye, they know I have my own career and even if I didn't, why am I now just this thing because I am married to someone who plays a sport?'

And while fans might think WAGs is a specialist subject for the players, they would have been shocked by the exploits of the England manager who had an array of WAGs all on his own; his girlfriends included Ulrika Jonsson, the FA's Faria Alam as well as Nancy Dell'Olio. The likeable Swede became England's first foreign boss and led the Three Lions to the last eight at all three of his tournaments in charge — the 2002 and 2006 World Cups plus Euro 2004 but while his persona seemed calm and sedate, his relationships off the park with Nancy Dell'Olio, Ulrika Jonsson and Faria Alam were far spicier. Eriksson regretted how his high-profile WAG antics hurt his reputation. Eriksson, speaking in an interview for the History channel, said: 'I thought I was prepared for England but I was not prepared for things outside football, my private life. I am not very proud that fans could probably name three of my former girlfriends. I don't think it damaged my football results. But my image outside football it damaged, yes.'

Eriksson added: 'My private life was not very private in England. In 2002, when it came out about a woman, well a Swedish one (Jonsson) I wondered what I should tell the players. It had nothing to do with football but I was their manager and we were going into a World Cup. I told them 'sorry' but one of players stood up and said: "Boss, welcome to England". That was it. I felt good. It was over.'

Eriksson regrets how England's World Cup dream ended at Germany 2006. The Three Lions were among the favourites and went home undefeated in open play after a quarter-final penalty shoot-out loss to Portugal. 'I still think we were not ready to win the World Cup in 2002 or Euro 2004. But we were ready in 2006. We should have done it. We played one hour, ten against 11, after Wayne Rooney was sent off. After the game I said something like: "Don't kill this young boy. You need him. You can kill me, because you don't need me any more."' Sven had already burned his bridges with the FA after falling prey to a tabloid sting by the 'fake sheikh' and the Portugal game was his last in charge of England.

WAGATHA CHRISTIE

Rebekah Vardy's decision to sue Coleen Rooney for defamation brought to court the full inside story of how the notorious, well-heeled, and Gucci/Prada/Hermes dressed WAGs operate behind the scenes: manipulating the media, determined to hit the spotlight and looking for lucrative spin-off endorsements.

Oh yes, there was the actual legal action brought by Mrs Vardy against Mrs Rooney, but did anyone really care about that? Absolutely not. It was "handbags" stuff their cliché ridden men would quote when there was a punch up on the field or on the training ground. It was more the designer handbag stuff in the court room as their 'ladies' lined up their best designer gear for the occasion. They might lose a ton of dosh to the shed load of lawyers, but they were determined to out do each other in the fashion stakes.

Here were two of the main characters in the history of the WAGs fighting out a bitter feud before an eager court room and wider watching audience, whose appetite for every gory detail of the WAGs egotistical life style emerged in the High Court. Did they follow the legal arguments? Not at all. They loved to see how much their football goalscoring husbands lavished on them in designer gear. At a time when the country was being told it would have to tighten its belt with soaring inflation, the women were showing off their best and most expensive best fitting belts.

The wives of two of the country's top goal-scorers of their generation, King Rooney of Manchester United and England's top scorer, and laugh-a-minute Vardy, were as much a laughing stock as their dear wives.

Vardy had lead humble little Leicester to the most unlikely Premier League title triumph of all time, followed it up by his club landing the FA Cup, but didn't lead from the front when his missus was in tears in the witness box, he remained in Leicester training and didn't ask for a day off to support his beleaguered wife, as it was far more important keeping in trim for the final games of a season in which his team were doing very little, in fact, nothing at all. But Jamie continued scoring his goals, and keeping in trim. Wise man, keeping out of the court room where Wayne was trapped listening to a multitude of indiscretions that ultimately brought his marriage to crisis point several times. Wayne could score off the pitch almost as much as he managed on it!

Meanwhile Rooney, now manager of already-relegated Derby, turned up to offer morale support to Coleen and hear all the gory details of his extra marital sex life, then give his own evidence, Vardy was miles away in the Midlands, seeing out the last few games of the season - no doubt glad he wasn't available for selection as part of Team Vardy and suffer similar unheralded humiliation like the other English goalscorer.

Besides the days of seemingly endless, fascinating, gormless inside information into the machinations of the nation's leading WAGs and Rooney's apparently endless shagging around with everyone from prostitute grannies to girls he picked up in nightclubs, there was also the fashion, the glamour, the Housewives of Cheshire meets the Housewives of the Midlands wanting their own fame and fortune, and in some cases demanding it!

Little wonder Beck's (Rebekah had to be shortened to Becks, didn't it?) agent begged her not to sue Coleen. Throughout her career, Caroline Watt, the PR agent, might have been well-known to those in the media, but few had heard of the poor woman - until now. Suddenly Caroline became a leading character in the court room drama playing a vital off-stage role between the warring WAGs.

Caroline must have pleaded long and hard for her client to take her advice and stay out of the court room, no doubt with the good intentions of protecting Beck's reputation. Little did she appreciate just how much it would affect her own life, although she should have realised she would be dragged into the whole sordid affair as Vardy's accomplice. Friends of the former air hostess were keen to let the media know that while she was initially supportive of her client after Coleen accused her of leaking stories, she quickly became alarmed when the row escalated into legal action that would ultimately push her centre stage.

Caroline Watt has been in the industry long enough to know how quickly legal action can run away from the party bringing it and land them in the dock as much as those they accuse, so it was a no-brainer to try to dissuade Becks from pursuing this illogical course.

Unfortunately Mrs Vardy believed that the only way to get Coleen to back down was to threaten legal action, and when that failed, and seemingly a few rounds of trying to sort it out amicably came to nothing, they were heading for the High Court and all that would entail.

Vardy was determined to get her apology from Coleen at any cost, but couldn't have realised how much it would cost. And that was not the estimated £3million in legal fees at stake. But the reputational cost. She just kept going and going as Coleen called her bluff in an out of court in a game of high stakes poker.

Becks was warned it was going to get expensive, but the old man could afford it, he was earning a fortune as a top Premier League star, albeit not at one of the most glamorous clubs, but he had enough endorsements on top of a decent salary, to be able to swallow the costs irrespective of how eye watering they might seem to the average worker in this country.

There was ample damaging correspondence between Watt and Vardy but Becks was on a runaway train, showing all her WAG 'front' and there was nothing Caroline could do about it.

Having spent so many years advising Becks, Watt eventually became her friend and confidante - the first person she turned to for gossip and back stabbing, which at first was very much in private, but the court case brought it all into the public domain, and it was so detailed, it was in the 'you-cannot-believe-it' category.

Becks accepted in court documents that Caroline may have leaked stories to *The Sun*, but claimed that this was without her knowledge. She was accused in court of betraying Mrs Watt by 'throwing her under the bus'. WhatsApp messages emerged showing that Mrs Watt admitted giving the newspaper a story about Coleen crashing her 4x4 car in Washington DC. It also emerged that Mrs Watt, who no longer works for Vardy and was unable to give evidence due to illness, also had a conversation with her about selling details about ex-Leicester City footballer Danny Drinkwater being arrested for drink-driving in 2019.

Rebekah Vardy's determination to win the High Court battle had taken its toll. It would not have been a pleasant catch up when Jamie got home from training, following her hard shift in the witness box of the High Court, to catch up on tales of selling stories about team-mates. How on earth would his current team-mates trust him not to pass on salacious gossip to his wife, who in turn would tip off her PR, who in turn would sell stories to *The Sun*?

The Vardy's are worth £12 million, so they can afford the legal fees, but the damage to their status as one of the game's golden couples looks damaged beyond repair. A Hollywood filmmaker was planning to make a movie about their rise to fame, especially Jamie's elevation from a part time footballer and tool maker to the heights of the national sport - it looked like it would need a new script and perhaps more of a script writer who can turn their hand to more than just the football.

Jamie had set up the V9 academy to find non-league football talent, which became the subject of a Sky TV series – but its Instagram page had not been updated for nearly a year, and it was clear that you might think twice about sending your son or daughter to such an establishment after all of this. At least Jamie scored for Leicester City in a 3-0 win over Norwich City and followed that up with a couple more in his next game - he was on fire, while poor Wayne Rooney was burning up on the bench in the High Court, no doubt not itching to get onto the field of play!

Wayne's numerous escapades off the field almost broke up their marriage, Coleen confessed for the first time. Just to emphasise the High Court was more a Jester Court, than there to judge on a defamation case.

So what was the Wagatha Christie trial all about and why did it get both parties so hot under their designer collars that ended up in high court? Well, Coleen shared a social media post in October 2019 accusing Becky of being behind leaks. Becky, 40, denies this and sued for libel.

After numerous stories had appeared in the tabloids that Coleen Rooney had only told a few close confidantes about she sought revenge. Coleen had her suspicions about who was leaking the stories to the press and so began a month long sting operation where she sent fake stories, which included her travelling to Mexico for a 'gender selection' procedure, a plan to return to TV and the basement of her home flooding, to only one account - that of Rebekah Vardy. Sure enough these stories made their way into the tabloids and Coleen then revealed the sting on Instagram, Twitter and Facebook writing, 'I have saved and screenshotted all the original stories which clearly show just one person has viewed them…

'It's…Rebekah Vardy's account.'

Vardy immediately denied leaking stories to the media, while Mrs Rooney defended the claim on the basis her post was "substantially true".

A comedian claimed to have created the 'Wagatha Christie' pun - now a global headline was shocked that three years after he first made the joke, it was used in the High Court and is 'in the mainstream'. Dan Atkinson, a writer and comedian who lives in Kent, said he first realised that the pun was catching on around 20 minutes after he first tweeted it on October 9th 2019, the day that Coleen revealed that she believed fellow WAG Rebekah had sold stories about her to the press. Writing in The Observer, Atkinson said he was staggered that people had monetised his phrase - with one entrepreneurial stylist reportedly making £50,000 in 24 hours after putting the comedy moniker on black t-shirts, saying he hadn't profited from his line.

TEAM ROONEY VS TEAM VARDY!

The warring WAGS had deep pockets and to hell with the costs as their loaded footballer hubbies picked up the tab. They made sure they had the best possible legal teams, and back up advisors, some of the country's finest media experts and legal minds as they went head-to-head in the celebrity trial of the decade. This was the Premier League of barristers and A list of advisors and supporting cast. Rebekah was even supported by a crisis manager who's an expert in online reputation and a burly body-guard in Jamie's absence - while Coleen had Hollywood's favourite barrister. Yes, it was no expense sparred. Little wonder it was billed as a £3million legal fees extravaganza, but with legal costs these days, it was probably double that amount.

In the blue corner was Hacked Off founder Hugh Tomlinson QC. No doubt top of the price list of barristers. But that was far from it in loading up the costs as Becks also had two glamorous members of the legal team, including one who was once named one of the 'sexiest lawyers' in the UK, and another who is a crisis manager experienced in online reputation.

In court, there was the need for a security guard to make sure those nasties from the media didn't intrude too much going in and coming out of the High Court, after all they might intrude on the 'photo opps', and that would be a shame after all the effort of those carefully selected outfits. Vardy had previously voiced her concerns about how security is important as she's faced threats ever since her feud with Coleen went public. She told *OK! Magazine* ahead of the 2018 World Cup that she and her family were bringing their own security to the games.

Yet, Coleen doesn't appear to have had a bodyguard by her entering court. Of course, with Wayne around who needs a body guard! The writers assigned to comment on proceedings in addition to their colleagues reporting on them, had a field day, as Wayne was likened to a burly bodyguard with his thick neck and bulging muscles, as one put it, he looked as though he had been pipped into his suit each morning.

Hollywood's favourite lawyer David Sherborne and rising legal mind Ben Hamer were the brains behind Coleen's defence.

TEAM VARDY

DR ROSA MALLEY

In Beck's legal team was Dr Rosa Malley, 37, an Associate in the Dispute Resolution team at top law firm Kingsley Napley. Rosa was a part of the Hacked Off campaign and specialises in reputation and media matters, who previously worked as a paralegal at top city law firm Mishcon de Reya, who led the High Court bid to stop Boris Johnson triggering Brexit. One of their barristers, Anthony Julius, acted for Princess Diana in her divorce from Prince Charles. The firm also represented Heather Mills in her divorce case against Paul McCartney, before separating 'amicably' from their client and acted for former Liberal Democrat Cabinet minister Chris Huhne when he faced allegations of perverting the course of justice by 'swapping' speeding points with his wife. Mr Huhne was later sentenced to eight months in prison. Rosa got her PhD studying the Representation of Women in British Politics at University of Bristol in 2011. She works in pre and post-publication for broadcast media, and has also worked in crisis management with politicians, sportspeople, celebrities and high profile criminal defendants. Before her legal career, Rosa worked in politics, as a researcher at the ThinkTank Institute for Government and as a Special Projects Manager for the Hacked Off campaign. She taught British Politics at Birkbeck, University of London. Especially for this case, Rosa's experience in online reputation and abuse on social media was essential.

CHARLOTTE HARRIS

Like rose, Charlotte, 44, worked at Hacked Off and for eminent law firm Mishcon de Reya. Described as 'one of the most sought out privacy lawyers in the land' she boasts a client base of 'MPs, celebrities, PR experts, sports agents, sports people'. In 2013, she married investment banker James Burr, their wedding was a star-studded events attended by the likes of Hugh Grant, MP Tom Watson, MP Chris Huhne, and Max Clifford. At the wedding millionaire former Energy Secretary Chris Huhne enjoyed his last night of liberty before he was sentenced the next day at Southwark crown court to eight months' imprisonment. Writing in the Diary column for the New Statesman at the time, Mr Watson said he 'entertained' the gathering of celebrities, MPs, bankers and high-

ly remunerated senior Mishcon staff with a kara-
oke rendition of the new wave anthem 'Teenage
Kicks'. She was named one of the country's
sexiest lawyers in 2015 in a list put together by
the website Legal Check. Charlotte has appeared before Parliamentary Select Committees
throughout her career, including the Leveson
Inquiry and was described as a 'force of nature
and always ready for a fight' by Chambers and
Partners High Net Worth Guide in 2020.

HUGH TOMLINSON QC

A top-flight privacy silk who has launched doz-
en of battles with the press in his four decade
career. The Leeds-born, Oxford-educated lawyer advocated successfully in a claim against a
journalist and author after she made false allegations that Roman Abramovich bought Chelsea
FC on Vladimir Putin's orders, one of several
lawyers representing Russian oligarchs whose
ethics were questioned in parliament by the
Conservative MP Bob Seely following Russia's
invasion of Ukraine. He represented Jeremy
Clarkson's ex-wife Alex Hall when he tried to
- but dropped - efforts to stop her claiming they
had an affair during his later marriage. He successfully represented Prince Charles who sought
to stop the publishing of his Hong Kong travel
diaries, saying public interest justifications were
'far-fetched'. He won substantial damages for
Christopher Jefferies after press coverage in-

correctly associated him with the murder of his tenant Joanna Yeates in 2010. A year later he co-founded Hacked Off, the group campaigning for tighter media regulation, which he now chairs, and which has backers such as Hugh Grant and Steve Coogan. He was born in Woodhouse in Leeds where he went to Leeds Grammar School and then Balliol College, Oxford, leaving with the top first in PPE. He took up philosophical studies at Sussex University before going to the University of Paris in 1977. In 2000 he was a founding member of Matrix Chambers in London.

NICOLA MCLEAN

The fellow WAG had thrown her support behind Becks several times - once stating that she is 'not as private' as she is considered while also insisting she is not interested in the fame game.

CAROLINE WATT

Friend and agent, Caroline featured in some of the preliminary hearings, despite not being a party to the claim or giving evidence at the trial. The former Virgin Atlantic air hostess who has been Rebekah's agent for the past seven years, helping to build her profile in the national media. Reports that she no longer represents her following the controversy were dismissed as inaccurate with her remaining close to Becks professionally and personally. Married to former footballer Steve Watt, who played briefly for Chelsea, making one Premier League appearance for two minutes in 2005, and Swansea City. Currently manager of Kent non-league side Hythe Town. They have two children. After leaving the airline industry, she began working as an agent in entertainment, developing a reputation for her communication skills and ability to network. Formerly employed by talent agency The Frontrow Partnership she left in 2019 to go it alone and took her main client and close friend, Becks with her and credited with building Becks public profile by ensuring that she regularly featured in the national media and brokered the deal for her to appear on the hit reality TV show *I'm A Celebrity. Get Me Out Of Here!* in 2018. Started representing the high-pr in 2015, when her Jamie shot to fame. She is a regular at the Vardy's Lincolnshire home and socialises with Becks, attending glitzy parties and bars. Her other clients include the former Page 3 girl Nicola McLean.

TEAM ROONEY

DAVID SHERBORNE

Coleen's legal team is well-versed in the world of celebrity. David Sherborne, 53, dubbed 'Hollywood's favourite lawyer', was lead counsel for victims of press intrusion in the Leveson inquiry, and represented Johnny Depp in his libel suit against *The Sun*. In November 2020, the High Court ruled that Depp had lost his case. In September 2020, Sherborne was dropped from the Duchess of Sussex's legal team in her case against The Mail on Sunday following an early setback. Sherborne's previous clients include Princess Diana, Melania Trump, Sir Paul McCartney, Sienna Miller, Kate Moss and Harry Styles. His father was a QC. He is seen as a 'rebel' due to his apparent fondness for the limelight. A former colleague told The Times: 'He likes to present a fun, outgoing persona and is very limelight-seeking. All the other barristers in chambers were hyper-critical of him breaking the rules.' Tattler and Evening Standard both commented he is 'so handsome' that he could be a celebrity himself. The twice-married barrister was revealed to be having an affair with a member of Lord Leveson's junior counsel, Carine Patry Hoskins, in 2013. Ms Hoskins, dubbed the 'thinking man's Pippa Middleton' was Lord Leveson's number two, while Mr Sherborne was defending Hugh Grant and other hacking victims.

BEN HARMER

There was a rare moment of light relief amidst fierce cross-examination when Mr Sherborne mentioned that his junior, Ben Hamer, 29, was 'very adept at searching online through social media on his phone.' Rebekah shot back, without smiling: 'I know, Mr Hamer follows me on Twitter' to laughter in the court. He has previously aided Kristen Bell and Dax Shepard and acted for the claimant in 'Blackledge v Person(s) Unknown' where libel and harassment damages of £70,000 were awarded against the Defendant. The Durham University graduate was first called to the Bar in 2017 at Lincoln's Inn, where he was a Lord Bowen and Lord Denning scholar. Accomplished at a young age, he was presented with the Benjamin Franklin House Literary Prize for his work on free speech and fake news. He provides pre-publication advice to various publications such as *The Times* and *The Sunday Times* as well as publishers HarperCollins and Bloomsbury. He is security cleared to SC level. Ben began as a tenant at 5RB after successful completion of pupillage at Chambers. His supervisors were Adam Wolanski QC, Jonathan Barnes QC, Richard Munden and Adam Speker QC. As an undergraduate, he edited Palatinate, where he won the Hunter Davies Prize for Student Journalism.

WAG PALS

When the story first broke Coleen thanked her fans and said there 'are a lot of really good people' in the world in an Instagram story in February 2022. Along with her devoted fans, there was public support from Danielle Lloyd, who came forth with similar claims about Vardy leading to a row between the pair on social media in 2019. Danielle made a thinly-veiled dig at Rebekah after weighing in on the libel row during an episode of This Morning. There were reports that many of the WAGs had distanced themselves from Becks, 'scrutinising' past conversations with her, following the fallout from her feud with Coleen. Following Mrs Lloyd's appearance on This Morning, Becks was quick to retaliate, as she took to Twitter to claim that the TV personality's admission was 'utter b******s' and their feud was sparked by her refusal to try and find Mrs Lloyd a man following her split from Jamie [O'Hara]. She wrote: 'Danielle Lloyd making false claims on @thismorning that we have had 'similar run-ins' is utter b****cks. She is just fuming that I 'didn't get Jamie recruiting' for her like she asked me to...'

THE JUDGE

MRS JUSTICE STEYN

Mrs Justice Steyn was appointed in 2019 and sits in the Queen's Bench Division - the part of the High Court which deals with defamation, personal injury and breach of contract claims. Other prominent cases she has heard include Arron Banks' libel claim against journalist Carole Cadwallader and the FDA union's unsuccessful legal challenge over Boris Johnson's decision to support Priti Patel following bullying accusations. Daughter of former Law Lord Lord Steyn, she covered a variety of cases as a barrister, including a case over the expansion of Heathrow airport.

TIME LINE

September 2017 to October 2019 - *The Sun* runs a number of articles about Coleen Rooney, including exclusives that she travelled to Mexico to look into baby 'gender selection' treatment, a plan to revive her TV career and the flooding of her basement.

October 9, 2019 - Coleen uses social media to accuse Rebekah of selling stories from her private Instagram account to the tabloids. Coleen said she had spent five months trying to work out who was sharing information about her and her family based on posts she had made on her personal social media page. After changing her profile so only Rebekah Vardy could see her page, she planted a series of 'false' stories which also made it into the tabloid press. She then shocked the social media world by accusing Rebekah Vardy of passing on the fake stories.

Rebekah, then pregnant with her fifth child, denied the allegations and says various people had access to Rooney's Instagram over the years. She was 'so upset' later adding: 'I thought she was my friend but she completely annihilated me.'

For a few years now someone who I trusted to follow me on my personal Instagram account has been consistently informing The SUN newspaper of my private posts and stories.

There has been so much information given to them about me, my friends and my family - all without my permission or knowledge.

After a long time of trying to figure out who it could be, for various reasons, I had a suspicion.

To try and prove this, I came up with an idea. I blocked everyone from viewing my Instagram stories except ONE account. (Those on my private account must have been wondering why I haven't had stories on there for a while.)

Over the past five months I have posted a series of false stories to see if they made their way into the Sun newspaper. And you know what, they did! The story about gender selection in Mexico, the story about returning to TV and then the latest story about the basement flooding in my house.

It's been tough keeping it to myself and not making any comment at all, especially when the stories have been leaked, however I had to. Now I know for certain which account / individual it's come from.

I have saved and screenshotted all the original stories which clearly show just one person has viewed them.

It's ....Rebekah Vardy's account.

coleen_rooney ✔ · Follow

coleen_rooney ✔ This has been a burden in my life for a few years now and finally I have got to the bottom of it....

1m

♡ ◯ ⬆   🔖

24 likes

Log in to like or comment

Rebekah Vardy ✔
@RebekahVardy

@ColeenRoo

As I have just said to you on the phone, I wish you had called me if you thought this. I never speak to anyone about you as various journalists who have asked me to over the years can vouch for. If you thought this was happening you could have told me & I could have changed my passwords to see if it stopped. Over the years various people have had access to my insta & just this week I found I was following people I didn't know and have never followed myself. I'm not being funny but I don't need the money, what would I gain from selling stories on you? I liked you a lot Coleen & I'm so upset that you have chosen to do this, especially when I'm heavily pregnant. I'm disgusted that I'm even having to deny this. You should have called me the first time this happened 🤍

The public dispute made headlines around the world, with the hashtag #WagathaChristie trending. Coleen Rooney, now 36, accused Rebekah Vardy, 40, of leaking 'false stories' about her to the press in an Instagram post Shortly after Coleen's public accusation, Rebekah - who was pregnant and on holiday in Dubai at the time - denied any involvement (above)

February 13, 2020 - In a tearful appearance on ITV's *Loose Women*, the stress caused Becks to have severe anxiety attacks and she 'ended up in hospital three times'. Coleen said in a statement that she does not want to 'engage in further public debate'.

June 23, 2020 - Becks launches libel proceedings against Coleen. Her lawyers allege she has 'suffered extreme distress, hurt, anxiety and embarrassment as a result of the publication of the post and the events which followed'.

November 19-20, 2020 - First High Court hearing in London. A judge ruled Coleen's October 2019 post 'clearly identified' Rebekah as being 'guilty of the serious and consistent breach of trust'. Mr Justice Warby concluded the 'natural and ordinary' meaning of the posts was that Rebekah had 'regularly and frequently abused her status as a trusted follower of Coleen's personal Instagram account by secretly informing *The Sun* of Coleen's private posts and stories'.

February 8-9, 2022 - A series of explosive messages between Rebekah and her agent Caroline

Watt - which Coleen's lawyers allege were about her - are revealed at a preliminary court hearing. The court is told Rebekah was not referring to Coleen when she called someone a 'nasty bitch' in one exchange with Ms Watt. Coleen's lawyers seek further information from the WhatsApp messages, but the court is told that Ms Watt's phone fell into the North Sea after a boat she was on hit a wave, before further information could be extracted from it.

February 14 - Coleen is refused permission to bring a High Court claim against Ms Watt for misuse of private information to be heard alongside the libel case. A High Court judge, Mrs Justice Steyn, said it was brought too late and previous opportunities had not been taken.

April 13 - Ms Watt is not fit to give oral evidence at the upcoming libel trial, the High Court is told as the case returns for another hearing. Vardy's agent revokes permission for her witness statement to be used, and withdraws her waiver which would have allowed Sun journalists to say whether she was a source of the allegedly leaked stories.

April 29 - Rebekah 'appears to accept' that her agent was the source of allegedly leaked stories, Coleen's barrister David Sherborne tells the High Court. He argues that a new witness statement submitted by Rebekah suggests Ms Watt was the source but Rebekah claims she 'did not authorise or condone her'. Rebekah's lawyer Hugh Tomlinson said the statement did not contain 'any change whatever in the pleaded case', with her legal team having no communication with Ms Watt.

PRE-TRIAL HEARING

Coleen "pointed the finger" at Rebekah as "the villain" who leaked stories to the press about her private life, the High Court first heard, back in November 2020. At the High Court, Vardy's barrister, Hugh Tomlinson QC, said Coleen's posts were an "untrue and unjustified defamatory attack... published and republished to millions of people". He said the row had been trivialised in the media as "wag wars" but "the impact on Mrs Vardy was not trivial".

Coleen planted three false stories on her Instagram stories blocking all users except for Becks account. Court documents said the three fake stories that appeared in *The Sun* consisted of Coleen travelling to Mexico to "see what this gender selection is all about", returning to TV, and the basement flooding in her house. On a Twitter post, she wrote: "I have saved and screenshotted all the original stories which clearly show just one person has viewed them.

"It's .... Rebekah Vardy's account."

Mr Tomlinson said Coleen's social media post made it clear that the person accused of leaking the stories "is Rebekah Vardy, the finger is being pointed at her, as the villain, the person, the someone, the one person". The Twitter backlash led some social media users to link Mrs Vardy with "the disappearance of Madeline McCann", and joke she was the new leader of the so-called Islamic State group, the barrister added. Mr Tomlinson wrote that the accusations had made Mrs Vardy feel suicidal, she had taken three trips to the hospital due to anxiety, and had fears she would lose her baby due to the stress of the situation. The written statement claimed husband Jamie had also been the subject of ridicule, with opposition supporters shouting taunting chants such as "Becky Vardy's a grass". Mrs Rooney's legal team claims Mrs Vardy "was in fact responsible for consistently passing on information about the defendant's private Instagram posts and stories to *The Sun*".

David Sherbourne, representing Mrs Rooney, stated in written submissions the message readers would take away from Mrs Rooney's tweet was "it was Rebekah Vardy's account that was the source of private stories about the defendant appearing in *The Sun* - not Rebekah Vardy herself". He added: "The fact that these sting operation stories also then appeared in *The Sun*... is the reason why the defendant published the post which is the subject of this claim."

Mr Tomlinson said both Mrs Vardy and Mrs Rooney had agreed for a "stay" of proceedings until February, so there could be "one final attempt to resolve the matter without the need for a full trial". Neither Mrs Rooney nor Mrs Vardy attended the preliminary hearing in London. At the hearing, Mr Justice Warby was asked to determine the "natural and ordinary" meaning of Mrs Rooney's posts.

Later in these drawn out proceedings, Rebekah said it was "war" after Coleen publicly accused her of leaking stories, a court heard. With the trial due to start in May, and a two-day hearing to decide what evidence can be used when that comes around, the High Court heard that WhatsApp messages between Mrs Vardy and her PR and friend Caroline Watt had been disclosed ahead of the trial. What's in those messages was discussed in court. On the day Mrs Rooney, the wife of former England star Wayne, published a post on Twitter which ended, "It's.......... Rebekah Vardy's account", Mrs Vardy sent a message to Ms Watt, stating: "That's war." The messages also revealed Mrs Vardy referred to Mrs Rooney and her husband Wayne with offensive language. One non-expletive term called Mrs Rooney "nasty".

Coleen's lawyers had previously claimed that Becks leaked information to *The Sun* newspaper either directly or through Ms Watt "acting on her instruction or with her knowing approval". In written arguments, Mrs Rooney's barrister David Sherborne said: "From the outset, Mrs Vardy has always claimed that neither she nor Ms Watt were involved in the leaking of private information from Mrs Rooney's Instagram account. The recent disclosure has shown that this is emphatically not the case," he added - referring to those WhatsApp messages.

According to Coleen's written case, messages between Becks and Ms Watt in January 2019 showed them discussing a post on Mrs Rooney's private Instagram where her car had been damaged. Mrs Vardy told Ms Watt she "would love to leak those stories x". Mr Sherborne said Ms Watt was later responsible for the leak of the story to the newspaper, with Mrs Vardy's approval. After the story was published in *The Sun* Mrs Rooney tweeted it was "sad" someone who followed her was "betraying" her. According to written submissions, while discussing the tweet in a private WhatsApp conversation, Ms Watt told Mrs Vardy "It wasn't someone she trusted. It was me", in a message accompanied by a laughing emoji. In written arguments Mrs Rooney's barrister said this "conspicuously elicits neither surprise, contradiction or criticism from Mrs Vardy, who was plainly aware and approved of this leak".

Mr Sherborne said Mrs Rooney had brought a claim against Ms Watt for misuse of private information, which Ms Watt denies. He added that Mrs Rooney's legal team had wanted more information from the WhatsApp messages between Mrs Vardy and Ms Watt, but said Ms Watt's phone had "regrettably" fallen into the North Sea after a boat she was on hit a wave, shortly after the last court hearing. "[It was] most unfortunate, because it was only a short time after the court ordered that the phone should be specifically searched," he said.

Hugh Tomlinson QC, representing Becks, said the denied allegations have caused her "huge damage and distress". In written arguments, the barrister said the information and messages disclosed "provides no evidence that the claimant leaked the three fake posts". He said Mrs Rooney "relies upon selective and incomplete WhatsApp exchanges... conveniently ignoring the messages which demonstrate beyond doubt that the claimant was not responsible for leaking the defendant's private information to *The Sun*".

In further WhatsApp messages between her and Ms Watt, Mrs Vardy said she had supported Mrs Rooney and suggested it was Mrs Rooney's own PR who had leaked stories. Ian Helme, for Ms Watt, said she had given "clear and consistent" denials against the claim for misuse of private information. The barrister said in written arguments that it was not only Mrs Vardy's Instagram account that had viewed the post about Mrs Rooney's car, adding that the incident also took place in public. "It is difficult to see how there could be said to be any reasonable expectation of privacy in relation to such information," Mr Helme said. He later said that Mrs Rooney's lawyers had taken "an extremely aggressive" approach and added it can be inferred that Mrs Rooney's primary concern is "public opinion, or vindication".

Rebekah was not referring to Rooney when she called someone an expletive in a message to her agent, the court heard. On the second day of a two-day hearing, Mrs Vardy's barrister said the "nasty" message was "about someone else" as proceedings continued to decide what evidence could be used in the May trial. The judge was told many of these messages were not supposed to be released but a software glitch meant they could be read by her rival's legal team and they want them to be included in the upcoming trial. They include the key message "I would love to leak those stories", from Mrs Vardy, about Coleen's Instagram posts. Mrs Rooney's lawyers have previously claimed that Mrs Vardy had leaked information to *The Sun* newspaper either directly or through Ms Watt "acting on her instruction or with her knowing approval". In court, her barrister David Sherborne had said those messages "reveal that Mrs Vardy and Ms Watt are responsible for the leaking". But now, Mrs Vardy's lawyer, Mr Tomlinson insisted they were "selective", and had "precisely the opposite effect". He also said a text in which she referred to someone as a "nasty" expletive was "not a passage about Mrs Rooney".

The barrister quoted messages from Mrs Vardy to Ms Watt in which she said she was "offended" that Mrs Rooney thought she was the person who had leaked the information. He added: "If one reads these messages in full, what one sees is that Mrs Vardy expresses shock at being accused and she is here communicating with the person that Mr Sherborne says is her co-conspirator. These are obviously candid personal messages, and if she was really concerned - 'Oh, this is terrible, we have been found out' - then it would have been completely different."

Coleen was also bringing a claim against Ms Watt for misuse of private information and is asking for it to be joined to the libel case. Mr Sherborne told the court that if Mrs Vardy wins her claim on the basis that she was not the person who leaked the information, then Mrs Rooney will be left without "vindication" unless she is able to bring the claim against Ms Watt as part of the same case. David Sherborne also said that Mrs Rooney's lawyers wanted further information from the WhatsApp messages between Mrs Vardy and Ms Watt, but were told Ms Watt's phone had fallen into the sea after a boat she was on hit a wave, shortly after the last hearing. "[It was] most unfortunate, because it was only a short time after the court ordered that the phone should be specifically searched," he said. Mr Tomlinson told the court: "That is what happened. Mrs Vardy was not present when that happened. She [Ms Watt] was on holiday, she lost her phone."

Mrs Vardy's lawyers have opposed the application to add the claim against Ms Watt to the libel case, saying in written arguments the claim "could have been brought 15 months ago".

Ian Helme, representing Ms Watt, also opposed the application and previously said she has given "clear and consistent" denials against the claim for misuse of private information.

Coleen was refused permission to bring a High Court claim against Rebekah's agent. She was ordered by the judge to pay £65,000 towards Ms Watt's legal costs following the unsuccessful attempt. However, the judge gave the go-ahead for Mrs Rooney to amend her defence case, to include an allegation that Rebekah Vardy, through Ms Watt, provided information to *The Sun* about an unnamed professional footballer. She also gave permission for disclosure of WhatsApp messages between Mrs Vardy and Ms Watt during the relevant period, and allowed Mrs Rooney's application for an order that both parties make a joint request for information to Instagram.

Mrs Rooney asked for permission to bring an "additional claim" against Ms Watt for misuse of private information and wanted it to be heard alongside the libel case. Her lawyer David Sherborne told the court Coleen Rooney would be left without "vindication" unless that could happen. Mrs Vardy's lawyers opposed the application to add the claim against Ms Watt to the libel case. Mrs Justice Steyn refused permission for the additional claim against Ms Watt and refused permission for it to be heard alongside the libel trial.

As the trial drew closer Rebekah "appeared to accept" that her PR was the source of leaked stories about Coleen, according to Mrs Rooney's barrister. David Sherborne claimed that Becks believes Caroline Watt may have been the source of the stories. In written submissions to the High Court, Mr Sherborne said that Mrs Vardy's new statement, provided, "suggests Ms Watt was the source of the leak but claims that Mrs Vardy 'did not authorise or condone her'".

"It now appears... that she too 'believes' that Ms Watt is the source," Mr Sherborne added. He added that the "collapse of Mrs Vardy's case over the last day has been remarkable". Mr Sherborne told the court that as of the evening of 27 April 2022, "in an abrupt change of position", that Rebekah Vardy "appears now to accept Mrs Rooney's case, that Caroline Watt... was the conduit" by which stories were leaked to *The Sun* newspaper. "It has become undeniably obvious that Ms Watt is the source and Mrs Vardy, true to form says 'it wasn't me, I didn't realise and I didn't know anything about what was going on'." He added that Mrs Vardy "says 'how awful it is to be betrayed'... That is exactly what Mrs Rooney would say, that she has been betrayed by someone".

However, Hugh Tomlinson, representing

Rebekah, told the court that her new witness statement did not contain "any change whatever in the pleaded case". He added: "We simply don't know what the true position is in relation to Ms Watt. She's not communicating with anybody. She's not communicating with anybody on our side and we don't know what her position is."

In his written arguments, Mr Tomlinson said there had "been important developments that have occurred" since Mrs Vardy gave her first written statement, but did not explain what they were. He continued: "These are all matters that are relevant to the proceedings and the issues that the court will need to determine."

"These developments are very recent. They were completely unexpected and outside the claimant's control...it has taken her time to process and consider the new information."

Caroline Watt was referred to at an earlier hearing after the High Court in London heard that WhatsApp messages between Mrs Vardy and Ms Watt had been disclosed. Texts heard in court included Mrs Vardy referring to someone, whose identity is disputed, as a "nasty" expletive. The court had previously heard that Caroline Watt's phone had "regrettably" fallen into the North Sea before further information could be extracted from it for the case. Ms Watt had been expected to give evidence at the upcoming trial, however, the High Court was told she was "not fit" to give evidence at a hearing earlier this month.

THE COURT CASE

Coleen arrived at court in a surgical boot alongside her husband - reminiscent of when Wayne injured his foot before the 2006 World Cup, the same tournament where the England "Wags" first exploded on to the scene in a big way amid blaze of tabloid stories. Journalists queued to get inside courtroom No 13 for this intriguing celebrity WAG case. Becks, sat at the front left bench with her hair in a bun and wearing a blue dress, while Coleen, wearing a black jacket, sat at the front right bench.

As if to emphasise that this trial was more Jester Court than High Court the opening day included, as an amusing aside, one of the most bizarre issues the judge and jury were likely to hear - the size of Peter Andre's manhood. Becks, though, was 'deeply sorry' for describing it like a 'chipolata'.

But the main course was far more serious. Becks feared she would lose her baby when Coleen made her allegations and 'will never forgive' her for 'ruining my pregnancy'.

Mr Tomlinson said the affair and subsequent libel case had garnered huge press coverage and had become a source of "entertainment" in the media, but, he added, "This is far from being an entertaining case. It has been profoundly distressing and disturbing." Mr Tomlinson added: "[Mrs Vardy] needs to be able to clear her name through this case, so she can move on from this terrible episode." He said that as a result of Mrs Rooney's post, Mrs Vardy - who was seven months pregnant at the time - and her family were subjected to abuse, including posts saying she should die. Her lawyer said she 'had no choice' but to bring the libel claim against Coleen to 'establish her innocence and vindicate her reputation.

He described Coleen's famous Instagram sting as 'flawed', rather than a 'careful investigation' that produced 'irrefutable' evidence as she suggested. He claimed Coleen 'revelled' in comparisons to Miss Marple, Agatha Christie and the Scooby-Doo gang.

Rebekah denied leaking information to newspapers as she gave evidence in her libel case against Coleen. "I didn't give any information to a newspaper," Becks insisted, "I have been called a leak and it's not nice."

Under questioning from Coleen's barrister, David Sherborne, on this opening day of the trial, Becks agreed it was "upsetting" and "wrong" for someone to secretly pass on another person's information, adding that she respected people's privacy. Mr Sherborne then questioned Becky about a story she had once given to the News Of The World about her alleged sexual encounter with singer Peter Andre, clearly a move to tear down her earlier statement that she respected people's privacy and didn't engage with the media for her own purposes or payment.

Asked whether it was "respectful" of Andre's "right not to share this information" with the paper, she replied: "I was forced into a situation by my ex-husband to do this". She added: "It is something that I deeply regret".

Becks claimed she 'has no knowledge' of an incident that saw agent Caroline Watt's phone fall into the North Sea and 'doesn't know' if she was the leaker of Coleen's Instagram posts. The claim Rebekah was involved in 'conspiracy' and a 'campaign of deletion' of evidence is 'completely baseless".

Coleen's barrister told the court of a "widespread and significant destruction or loss of evidence" in this case. The loss of Becky's documents "must be concealment" he told the court in yet another significant twist in the entire story however Vardy's barrister Hugh Tomlinson described the claim as "completely baseless".

The court heard that Beck's agent, Caroline Watt, had lost her phone in the North Sea after it was hit by a wave before Coleen's team could see WhatsApp messages that could potentially help her case. Mr Sherborne told the court there had been "a concerted effort to ensure highly relevant and incriminating" documents didn't make it to court. He said a series of "most improbable events" had affected the disclosure of evidence, including Ms Watt's "poor unfortunate phone" falling into the sea "within days" of the court ordering that it should be searched for disclosure.

"What terrible luck," Mr Sherborne said. In a written submission, he added: "To borrow from Wilde, to lose one significant set of documents may be regarded as a misfortune, to lose two, carelessness, but to lose 10? That must be concealment."

Mr Tomlinson countered that it had not been suggested "that Becks was anywhere near the North Sea at the time" nor that she "knew anything about it". He added that there was a "credible, ordinary, boring explanation" behind media files on Mrs Vardy's WhatsApp account no longer being available. "It's a very well-known and common feature in everyone's life that from time to time electronic documents are lost for all kinds of reasons," he said, adding, "this is something that happens to us all, that sometimes documents are lost."

Coleen's barrister, David Sherborne, blindsided and confused the mum-of-five when he asked about Watt losing her phone in the North Sea days after she was ordered to turn it over. The lawyer asked: "We know that Miss Watt's phone is now in Davy Jones' Locker, don't we, Mrs Vardy?" Rebekah was clearly baffled. Then replied: "I'm sorry, I don't know who Davy Jones is." People in the court room burst into laughter, the judge explained it's an idiom for the bottom of the sea.

Despite that brief moment of levity, Becks left the witness box in tears following the jibes from Mr Sherborne. After complaints of poor form from Rebekah's lawyer Hugh Tomlinson, judge Mrs Justice Steyn rapped the barrister. She branded his jibes "unnecessary" and told him: "There's not really enough time for those comments in any event."

In a pre-trial hearing less than two weeks before the trial began, Coleen's barrister had claimed that Becks now "appears to accept" that Ms Watt was the source of leaked stories. Ms Watt denied being the source of the leaks and was deemed too ill to testify.

Coleen's barrister compared Beck's connection with Ms Watt in relation to the leaks as "like hiring a hit man or woman". He said: "Just because you're not the person who gets their hands dirty, doesn't mean you're not equally responsible." And went on to claim that Vardy 'had the means, motive and opportunity to leak stories about Coleen'.

Mrs Vardy, he stressed, "is just as responsible" for the stories being leaked even "if she doesn't pull the trigger". He said there had also been "numerous examples of the claimant and Ms Watt conspiring to pass private and personal information on to the press about other individuals".

However Mr Tomlinson said that if Ms Watt was the source of leaked stories, "that's not something that Mrs Vardy knew anything about" and she did not "approve of or authorise" her to do so. He told the court that Becks "had no choice" but to bring the libel claim against Mrs Rooney because she needed to "establish her innocence and vindicate her reputation".

Mr Tomlinson said that, if information had been leaked, "this was not something that was done with Mrs Vardy's knowledge or authority". He said there was "no information" in any evidence to demonstrate that Mrs Vardy had even viewed Mrs Rooney's Instagram posts during the alleged "sting operation".

The fake stories posted by Mrs Rooney included planning her return to TV, travelling to Mexico for a "gender selection" procedure and her basement flooding. With so much pride, huge egos, and reputations at stake on both sides, the onus was on the defendant, Coleen, to prove that it was in fact Becks who leaked the stories.

Mr Sherborne, acting for Coleen, told the court: "She's not here because she wants to be, she's here because she has to be."

Her investigation into the leaks was "deeply upsetting" for Mrs Rooney and made her feel "paranoid", he told the court. Coleen's barrister, David Sherborne, told the court the case hinged on 'betrayal' – whether it was by Rebekah who betrayed Coleen by leaking information to *The Sun* or Vardy's agent, Caroline Watt, who was responsible.

WhatsApp messages between Rebekah and her agent where Rebekah referred to Coleen as a 'c***' were re-read to the court. Becks had been 'jeered and heckled at football matches' and 'made the butt of endless jokes' since the allegations emerged. The court was adjourned for a second time after Rebekah put her head in her hands and sobbed: "There's been a lot of abuse."

But Becks was accused of lying after denying she set up paparazzi to take pics of WAGs during the 2018 World Cup. Vardy's claim that she sat behind Coleen at the 2016 Euros because they were the 'nearest seats available' was 'untrue', according to a new witness statement. 'Harry Maguire's fiancée Fern Hawkins was 'upset and embarrassed'.

DAY TWO

The second installment of the trial featured a tearful appearance in the witness box as Becks faced a grueling cross examination, WhatsApp 'gossip' about a mystery celebrity affair, more foul-mouthed text messages - all brought to an end by a fittingly dramatic fire alarm. Coleen publicly 'outed' Becks when she accused her of sharing three fake stories she had posted on her personal Instagram with *The Sun* as part of what she described as a social media 'sting' operation. Rebekah vehemently denied the allegation.

Today focused on Becks relationship with her agent Caroline Watt as "Becks' faced a barrage of accusations…. Becks and Ms Watt worked to improve the WAG's media coverage and plotted to leak several stories to *The Sun*. She was accused of telling her publicist Ms Watt to look at Coleen's private Instagram account through her own personal account, but denied that she ordered her to 'monitor' the page. Ms Watt once 'boasted' that a Sun journalist 'always writes nice stories' about Rebekah and 'does whatever I ask her'. It was 'standard practice' for Rebekah to give her publicist information to pass on to journalists, and that Ms Watt would do Rebekah's 'dirty work' for her. It was 'standard practice' for Rebekah to give her publicist information to pass on to journalists, and that Ms Watt would do Rebekah's 'dirty work' for her. Rebekah tried to leak model Danielle Lloyd's miscarriage to the media following a 'spat on Instagram' - an allegation which she has denied. She and Ms Watt discussed leaking a story about a female celebrity accused of cheating on her husband with a 'well-known footballer' - but Becks insisted that she was just 'joking'.

In one of the more humorous episodes of the day, 'Becks' claimed she was "distracted" by Gemma Collins "faceplanting" on *Dancing on Ice* when her agent Caroline Watt admitted in texts she'd tipped off the press about Coleen's 2019 car crash in Washington.

The court showdown was as much about the whodunnit on the leaking of Coleen's private `Instagram account, as the machinations of the WAGs off the field's shenanigans.

It emerged that 'Becks' shared information to the media about unrest in the Leicester camp and once tried to 'do the dirty' and spill the beans on unrest in the Leicester City dressing room when star winger Riyad Mahrez went 'on strike' and missed two days training - but denied she had leaked the story to *The Sun* and had been 'gossiping'.

In February 2018, Mahrez asked for a transfer but when a move to Manchester City fell through he stopped attending training. In a WhatsApp message to Watt, 'Becks' wrote: 'Mahrez not turned up for training again. The lads are fuming.' Watt suggested she contact TV reporter Rob Dorsett, who was one of the journalists covering the story for Sky Sports News. 'Becks' replied that she didn't want the story to 'come back on me'. Dorsett subsequently tweeted: 'I'm told Riyad Mahrez failed to report for #lcfc training this morning. He has now missed two training sessions and a game, so is technically in breach of contract and on strike. Sources say he is depressed after failing to get his move to #mcfc.'

Under cross examination from Coleen's barrister, she said: 'It was pretty much unheard of for a player to go on strike and not turn up for training.' She insisted, though, that the story of turmoil in the dressing room 'absolutely 100 per cent did not come from me'.

In the messages, Watt then suggested that she could 'tell someone' about Mahrez's no-show and Rebekah replied 'do it'. But she admitted that 'in a fleeting moment' it appeared from Watt's response that she was 'prepared to do her dirty work' for her. She insisted the information didn't come from Jamie. She said: 'the gossip was already out there.' She told the High Court that she was 'just gossiping' when messaging her agent.

'It was speculation of just bits of information that I had heard and overheard, and also read in the press before,' she said. She admitted: 'Yes, it doesn't look good there, I was gossiping about things that we already in the public domain. I was just gossiping. Her husband 'never discussed whether the lads were fuming',' she said, but she admitted that the message exchange with her agent 'doesn't read very well'. Mahrez eventually returned to training for Leicester but secured the transfer to Manchester City for £60m in the summer of 2018

She did admit, though, that "for a moment" she considered going to the press about a story involving Danny Drinkwater's drink-driving crash to *The Sun* newspaper because she didn't approve of drink driving and 'wanted paying' for any information that reached the Press. In May 2019, Drinkwater was banned from driving for 20 months and ordered to carry out 70 hours' community service after admitting drink-driving. He had two women passengers in the car and caused £50,000 of damage to the vehicle. By this stage, Drinkwater had left Leicester, joining Chelsea in 2017 for £35m and has this season been on loan at Reading. During five years at the King Power Stadium, a strong bond had formed between the players, forged in a failed promotion attempt from the Championship, before finally making it to the Premier League, surviving relegation and then winning the title.

In the title-winning season, 'Drinky' and 'Vards' were key members of the team that a strong unity within their dressing room. The pair were leaders in team bonding, such as the 'flying socks' game, which were randomly aimed at unsuspecting victims in the changing room, and 'a full-blown extravaganza' in Copenhagen that saw the squad required to dress as their favourite super hero on a trip to Denmark organised by goalkeeper Kasper Schmeichel. Drinkwater went as a Mutant Ninja Turtle, while Jamie was a White Power Ranger. Drinkwater is quoted as saying 'we all get along together', but even so, when he became newsworthy, after he crashed his car, it seems the former Manchester United youth player was just a story as far as Rebekah was concerned.

'Becks' admitted in court she told a reporter at *The Sun* about Drinkwater's arrest and that he had spent a night in the cells. 'Danny Drinkwater arrested... Crashed his car drunk with 2 girls in it … both in hospital one with broken ribs,' a message to Watt read, according to court documents. Rebekah also said: 'I want paying for this.' Later, it emerged the story had already come out. 'Holy F*** … I'm fuming I didn't give it to you earlier,' 'Becks' message pal and PR Caroline. 'Me too,' Watt replied. 'That would have been a fortune.'

Rebekah told the court that was correct but added Caroline also included 'laughing face' emojis. 'I realise how badly they read and again I apologise,' she told the court. 'But again, these are private conversations between two people... that knew each other's sense of humour.' Mr Sherborne asked if this was a joke or serious, and said Rebekah 'can't have it both ways'. Rebekah replied that in relation to her message exchange with Caroline about the Drinkwater story that 'it was something that wrongly I got involved with'. She apologised and that the 'messages were not good', adding it was about something that 'affected me very badly in the past'. She told the court she was 'deeply affected' by drink-driving as her ex-husband had 'killed two people'.

For Coleen, Mr Sherborne said: 'Mrs Vardy was a highly unreliable witness. Her evidence should be treated with the utmost caution. Its accuracy simply cannot be trusted.'

The barrister claimed he had proved that Rebekah had 'regularly and frequently' leaked information to *The Sun* about his client and others in her sphere. He said: 'Just because she [Vardy] was not the one who pulled the trigger on occasion, it does not mean she was not responsible.'

And he highlighted WhatsApp messages Vardy exchanged with Watt regarding Drinkwater, claiming they were an example of 'where she is trading money for private information'.

Story.....Danny Drinkwater arrested.

Becky

For what?

Miss Watt

Crashed his car drunk with 2 girls in it. Both in hospital with 2 broken ribs. He has been only just let out of the cells. I want paying for this

Becky

F**k someone already tipped it

Becky

"I'm fuming I didn't give it to you earlier

Becky

DAY THREE

Becks denied branding herself 'the unofficial leader of the WAGs' in a Sun interview about axing the 'sex ban' for England stars during Russia World Cup claiming that she was too busy 'washing her clothes in a sink' during the 2018 World Cup to have time to speak to journalists!

She also denied leaking information about Coleen's 2019 car crash in Washington DC to the media after seeing story on her private Instagram and claimed she 'doesn't really watch' television and asked 'who's Davy Jones?' while being questioned about alleged leaks and her publicist's North Sea incident.

Becks denied being behind the 'Secret Wag' column that included lurid claims of Chelsea 'love rats'. Becks was unable to explain what had happened to nine months of messages she exchanged with Ms Watt which disappeared. She was accused of 'using the anniversary of Coleen's sister's death as a peg to contact her after the WAG unfollowed her on Instagram' something that Coleen took up in her account of events.

In her witness statement, Rooney said: 'Going through the Instagram accounts of friends and family one by one and assessing whether or not you thought they were responsible for leaking information about you to *The Sun* was a horrible exercise. The leaks were consistent and they were coming from my own private Instagram account, as opposed to just wider information about my life, and therefore there was a relatively limited pool of possible suspects. I came to the conclusion that the account responsible clearly had a relationship with *The Sun* and it's journalists because it was only *The Sun* that was printing the 'exclusive' articles based upon information from my private Instagram account.'

Coleen said a message between Rebekah and her agent referencing her dead sister 'knocked me sick' when it was disclosed. Coleen wrote in her witness statement: 'While they were discussing her messaging me in order to cover her tracks, Becky says to Caroline Watt 'maybe I should say something about Rosie'. This is a reference to my sister who suffered with Rett Syndrome and passed away in 2013 at the age of just 14. The mere fact that Becky would suggest seeking to use Rosie's name in conversation with me in order to put me off the scent of suspecting Becky as the person responsible for leaking my private information to *The Sun* is really low and sad. It actually knocked me sick when I read that message from Becky to Caroline.'

Rebekah would 'regularly' message Coleen when there was press coverage about her, the High Court heard. Pointing out Rebekah was 'not in my circle', Coleen said: 'I felt like when she contacted me it was to try and get information out of me.' Rebekah's messages to her always came 'when something not nice was going on in my personal life', Coleen claimed. Rebekah's messages were 'generally nice', but added that 'towards the end its was a bit unusual,' describing Vardy as 'someone who was not that close to me... constantly checking in with me all the time.'

Coleen told how she offered 'an olive branch' to 'Becks' in a bid to end their bitter public dispute. Coleen said she made three attempts to bring their legal battle to a close as she believed it would 'benefit neither Becky nor myself'. But she said her efforts had all been 'in vain'.

In a written statement submitted to the court she said: 'I would like to highlight at the outset of this witness statement that I have sought to resolve this matter amicably on various occasions because I was of the view that the time, money, resources and efforts involved could be better spent elsewhere - particularly in light of the Covid-19 pandemic.' She told how she made three separate attempts to call a truce, the first in May 2020 before proceedings were issued. Coleen tried again after filing legal documents in October 2020 then made a further attempt in January 2021. But she said: 'The efforts I made were in vain' adding, 'I have no doubt that this litigation, whatever the outcome, will benefit neither Becky nor myself.

'I should, however, highlight that those attempts to compromise this dispute were not made due to any concern with the underlying merits or an absence of confidence in my position,' Rooney added, 'I was seeking to be pragmatic and to consider the bigger picture in order to enable both parties to move on with our respective lives – essentially an olive branch if you will. I have always been confident in the truth of what I posted on October 9 2019.She said Rebekah's WhatsApp conversations with her agent Caroline Watt, had 'only further reinforced my view on that'.

Rebekah leaked details of Wayne being caught drink driving with a woman he had met in a bar, Coleen said in court documents. Coleen told how she was left 'really hurt' after details of how she had moved out of the family home with her sons in the wake of the incident were made public. She said she felt 'as though someone that I trusted was betraying me at a very difficult time.' Coleen posted a picture of herself with her sons on her private Instagram account after her husband was pulled over by police as he drove home with single mother Laura Simpson. The following day *The Sun* newspaper published an article which said Coleen had 'dropped a heavy hint that she would keep the kids with her if she and Wayne do split'. It revealed how Coleen 'uploaded two poignant photos of the boys on her Instagram account and wrote: 'No matter where I am they always follow me, and I hope that lasts forever'.'

'Becks' 'fished' for information after the Rooney's' marital woes were leaked. In her written statement Coleen told how she exchanged WhatsApp posts with Rebekah over the next two days 'in which she checked in on how I was doing and even offered for me to stay at her house if I wanted to get away from things'. Coleen said: 'On the face of things, this was obviously a nice gesture, but I did think at the time that it was a bit over the top because Becky and I weren't particularly close friends.'

Coleen said in her witness statement: 'No other content had been uploaded to my social media platforms about the incident and I hadn't mentioned the marriage post to anybody else. It was obvious to me that a follower on my private Instagram account had leaked the post to *The Sun* and that the source of the marriage article was the marriage post. There was so much going on at that time that I didn't take any action or do anything about the leak but I definitely took note of it and was really hurt by it, particularly because I felt as though someone that I trusted was betraying me at a very difficult time.'

Coleen told how she believes Rebekah had been 'fishing for information' in previous exchanges between them. She said there had been discussions between the pair from August 2016 to February 2017 'in which she would directly ask me about topics involving me that had been mentioned in the press. For instance, she asked me about an attempted burglary at my house, about a potential midwife documentary and about my house build. At the time I just thought she was trying to be friendly but [I felt she] was a bit too keen. In hindsight, I do wonder whether her messages - and indeed all of the messages that she sent to me subsequently were just fishing for information to pass to the media.'

DAY FOUR

Coleen again favoured high-street over designer as she arrived at the High Court wearing a £69.99 blazer from Zara. She put on a casual display in a straight-fit blazer and matching trousers, paired with a simple t-shirt, ahead of the fourth day of the case. It was the second time Coleen donned the Spanish-brand, sporting a £32.99 printed dress on the second day of the trial with a single-button blazer made from eco-friendly fabric. 'Becks' arrived in a chic monochrome suit which she paired with a white blouse and £1,690 Givenchy handbag. In the style stakes Coleen favoured more low-key brands but couldn't resist taking part in the battle of the bags with a classic Chanel flap bag in white, costing £4,480. Still sporting a medical boot on her left leg following an injury, she stepped out in a pair of white statement Gucci leather loafers decorated with stars and bees worth £620.

Before the court heard from Coleen on Friday the 13th for the first time, 'Becks' finished her evidence after she broke down twice on the witness stand the day before.

Having given evidence for around 10 hours, and, at times becoming emotional in the witness box, 'Becks' barrister asked her about the comments - made in a kiss and tell story in the News of the World in 2004 - as the trial got underway. She claimed that she did not say many of the things presented in the article published about Peter Andre's manhood. Becks admitted, though, branding Peter's manhood a "chipolata" was one of her "biggest regrets" having made the comment in a 2004 kiss-and-tell story on the singer. She confessed that it was a "shameful" remark as she continued her evidence on day four about it. Becks told London's High Court: "The circumstances of that article I have gone into already which I am deeply sorry for. It's shameful and one of my biggest regrets.

'There's a lot of things in there that didn't come out of my mouth that were misrepresented in the circumstances around that article I'm deeply sorry for", adding 'It is not nice to read and I understand why this is being used and to me…'

Vardy said that as she was only 22 at the time she was still immature and not too clever dealing with a newspaper as powerful of the News of the World and revealed when asked if she has spoken to Andre about it since, said: 'I haven't spoken to him but I sent both his wife and him personal messages a couple of years ago.'

Andre has since spoken out about the claim, insisting his 'acorn' has 'grown into an oak'. Peter, 49, was forced to speak up yet again, though, about something he would rather have avoided. He was mercilessly mocked about his manhood for 15 years after Rebekah claimed he had the "smallest trouser equipment she's ever seen". Rebekah and Peter met just four months after she married her first husband, Mark Godden, and according to reports at the time, they had an affair. Rebekah claimed that her marriage was already shaky, and in the process of separation. Peter met Rebekah in a restaurant in 2001, and gave her his number, and the affair unfolded while she was working for a promotion firm. Rebekah said of the affair: "He was really sweet and led me upstairs. When we were in the room, he stripped me and took his top off. He had great muscles. I thought he was going to be a fantastic lover. Then he took his trousers off! He was the worst lover I've ever had. It wasn't even worth the train fare. Peter was tiny. The smallest trouser equipment I've ever seen. It was like a miniature chipolata."

Vardy claimed that she was "forced into a situation by my ex-husband" to do the interview. Becks was questioned in the High Court about the explosive and sexually explicit interview where she described a sexual encounter with Andre. Barrister David Sherborne showed an A3 print-out of the article to Becks before reading the headline: 'Peter's hung like a small chipolata, shaved, slobbery, lasts five minutes.'

Peter took to his social media to discuss this incident being brought up, stating: 'Fifteen years this has been going on and I kept quiet and I didn't say anything and I let everyone have their laugh and I let everyone say what they wanted to say. Yes, now she has gone to court and admitted that the story was made up and she did that because her ex-husband forced her to do it, fair enough. But put that all aside and just think how that feels, if a man had said this about her anatomy and made up something, you can use your imagination, saying something very unflattering, there would be absolute outrage. But because it has been said about me it's been the butt of all jokes, I've taken it for 15 years.

'I know some of you are gonna go, "get over it, don't say anything". You gotta understand when it goes on and on and being brought up, and even worse it's been brought up in the High Court and the lawyer is bringing it up having a go at her for bringing up something in News Of The World that went to four million people and then it's brought up in court that goes to a lot more than four million people, it's brought up again, and the only one that sits there and takes hit after hit about it is me.' He added that he's 'been laughing about it for a while' but wants people to consider 'how they would feel if it was the other way round.'

An insider told *OK! Magazine*: 'Pete is livid. This whole thing has been really hard on him and the family, but it's made him think about the wider story and that is that other people shouldn't be allowed to talk about others in this way. It's so discriminating to say this about a man, this would not be said about a woman. His children have been asking what the story is about, which is really difficult. He has no recollection of meeting this person, never mind anything else.' The Australian star – who has kids Amelia, eight, and Theo with wife Emily and Junior, 16, and Princess, 14, with ex-wife Katie Price – was devastated it was all brought up into the public domain once again. The source added: 'Pete wasn't told his name would be mentioned in a major court case and he feels it's totally wrong. This story has been regurgitated for 15 years and he's been biting his lip for 15 years. For someone else to talk about personal parts of his body is upsetting for him and his family. He's got children that go to school and can hear all of this. It shouldn't be allowed for someone to do this to another person. Thank God she's admitted it's a made up story.' Andre voiced his upset after the comments about his body were repeatedly brought up for 15 years, and he questioned how people can claim to care about 'mental health' and 'being kind' when he's been 'the butt of all jokes' for such a long time.

Rebekah insisted that she only discussed Coleen's private Instagram account with her agent Caroline 'a handful of times'. Rebekah explained that the publicist had access to her own Instagram account password from 2017 when the TV personality appeared on *I'm a Celebrity Get Me Out of Here!* under questioning from her barrister Hugh Tomlinson QC, 'Becks' said she 'didn't give it a second thought' that Caroline was able to see Coleen's private Instagram account. Asked if she was told by Ms Watt that she was looking at Coleen's account, Rebekah said: 'No she didn't', adding that it 'was not even on my radar' when asked if knew Ms Watt was 'monitoring' Coleen's account.

Rebekah admitted plotting to leaking information about Danny Drinkwater's drink-drive arrest to the media and sent the footballer a 'FFS' message after his 2019 car crash. Rebekah told her publicist Caroline that she 'wanted paying' for information about the former Leicester City player leaving police custody after his arrest. Earlier in the case she denied she actually wanted money for the tip. Drinkwater was banned from driving for 20 months and ordered to complete 70 hours of community service after pleading guilty to drink driving. Rebekah told her lawyer Mr Tomlinson that she sent Drinkwater a private message on Instagram asking: 'What have you done FFS Danny?'. The acronym 'FFS' stands for 'For F**k Sake' - earlier this week the court heard Rebekah explain this to Coleen's lawyer David Sherborne.

'Becks' denied being behind 'leaks' of stories about Riyad Mahrez, an unnamed celebrity 'cheating with a footballer', and Coleen's 2019 DC car crash.

Rebekah denied asking Drinkwater for his address so she could send paparazzi photographers and reporters around to his home.

'Becks' was also questioned about whether she conspired with her agent to leak a story about Coleen crashing her car in Washington DC to the media after spotting it on her private Instagram. The Court has heard how Caroline texted Rebekah admitting that she had given information about Coleen's crash in Washington DC to *The Sun* newspaper. Rebekah now said it 'appeared' that Caroline was the source of the story, but said she didn't reply to her text because she was too engrossed watching Gemma Collins' *Dancing On Ice* 'faceplant'.

Mr Tomlinson asked: 'Were you instructing Caroline Watt to go into the Instagram to obtain information to leak to *The Sun*?'

Rebekah replied: 'No, I wasn't'.

Rebekah was questioned in relation to a WhatsApp exchange with Carolyn in which they discussed Coleen's child allegedly not wearing a seat belt in a photo from Coleen's private

Instagram. Mr Tomlinson said that, in a text, Ms Watt said: 'It's on the private Instagram so can't do anything with it.'

She 'didn't know' what her agent was implying when she said about 'it's on her private Instagram so we can't do anything with it 'after spotting that one of the Rooney's children wasn't wearing a seatbelt.

He asked Rebekah what she understood Ms Watt to be saying at this point. 'I don't know, I didn't really give it much consideration or much thought,' 'Becks' replied, adding: 'I was probably doing the school run myself at that time.'

Mr Tomlinson asked: 'Did you think that Caroline was leaking stories from Coleen's private Instagram account?'

'No, I didn't,' she said.

Becks insisted she only discussed Coleen's private Instagram account with her PR agent Caroline 'a handful of times'.

A 2016 story claiming Wayne wanted Rebekah to keep a lower profile was described by the footballer as 'a load of bollocks'. The story in the Independent claimed Wayne told team-mate Jamie his wife was getting too much publicity and it was affecting team morale.

Rebekah told the court: 'Jamie was quite angry [about the story] that conversation never took place. I had a conversation with Mr Rooney on Facetime about it and he said it was a load of b*******.'

She added: 'I thought the media were trying to cause problems and stir up trouble, creating a drama and problems where they didn't exist.'

Rebekah told the court she was scared she was going to lose her baby in the days following Coleen's bombshell Wagatha post. She was seven months pregnant at the time, and was asked by her solicitors to export her WhatsApp messages onto her laptop on October 15, 2019, just six days after the post. Asked to describe her state of mind at the time, she sobbed as she said: 'Constant anxiety, panic attacks, and I was scared I was going to lose my baby.'

She denied deliberately deleting the information which the court has heard was lost during the export. Rebekah has denied ever purposefully deleting her WhatsApp messages after evidence 'went missing';

The court previously heard swathes of messages were unavailable because they had been accidentally wiped, while others did not show images, video, or audio they contained.

Mr Tomlinson asked: 'Have you at any stage deliberately deleted anything from your WhatsApp messages?'

'No, never', she replied.

Moments earlier she spoke of her emotional state at the time she was exporting her messages, during which she claims many were inadvertently deleted. She said: 'I wasn't very well, I was having constant panic attacks, anxiety, I was scared I was going to lose my baby.'

As Rebekah's lawyer closed her case, Mr Tomlinson asked her how she had found the experience of being cross-examined by Mr Sherborne. 'Exhausting, intimidating – I feel like I've been bullied and manipulated,' she said through tears. He asked her why she had continued with the case and again she became emotional as she said: 'I wanted to clear my name, not just for me, but for my family and my children.'

Collen has been guarded about making public comments regarding her inner-most feelings about her husband's numerous indiscretions. However there was no hiding place in the witness box of the High Court. Suddenly Coleen was no longer able to sweep it under the carpet. Both WAGs had to bare their souls to make their points and it was not very pleasant for their other halves, but it made fascinating reading for those given an insight into their private lives as never before, in a way not even seen in the glossy celebrity mags. For now Wayne was there every day, Jamie had yet to turn up but his time would come.

Coleen clearly didn't want to be in that witness box and had 'offered an olive branch' to Becks to stop her legal action but it was 'in vain'.

But Coleen was 'always been confident in the truth' of her social media "sting"'.

Yet, that is what they were in the High Court to resolve the issue of whether it was libel or not, and so the full graphic details of how Coleen meticulously planned 'Scousetrap' sting on Becks after becoming suspicious of her rival WAG when she began 'fishing for information' when they weren't even friends was the highlight of the day.

The now infamous Wagatha Christie plot was not 'plucked out of thin air' Coleen told the court, the room yet again packed, as she took to the stand. Coleen was to tell the court that her infamous 'Wagatha Christie' Instagram post was a 'last resort' and 'wasn't an attempt to get Rebekah trolled'.

Describing how her investigation began to gain momentum, Coleen said: 'There were a number of things that added up with the others. I didn't just pluck it out of thin air. I suspected this person was having a relationship with *The Sun* so I googled it, looked at past articles and saw the connection between Rebekah Vardy and *The Sun*. This thing was not just thought of overnight. I did think of it for a long time. As I've said I'm not one who just jumps on things. I was trying to get more information and put it together with the information I already had. I came up with Rebekah Vardy. There was no other person on my private Instagram who was in a position to give this information to *The Sun.*'

Coleen discussed a story which emanated from a private Instagram post featuring Wayne and the couple's children in pyjamas. She was upset when she saw a story she believed was based on the post. The key post led to the trial at the High Court, as Coleen accused Becks of leaking 'false stories' about her private life to the press. Vardy denied leaking stories to the media and sued Rooney for libel, while Coleen defended the claim on the basis her post was 'substantially true' and in the public interest.

Describing their relationship, Coleen said: 'I've never had a drink with Mrs Vardy. We've never socially interacted. We've met on a few occasions at football but we've never interacted socially. I've never picked the phone up to Rebekah Vardy. The only time I spoke to her on the phone was the day of the post.'

Leaks 'strained Coleen's relationships with fellow WAGs and those close to me who thought that I suspected them as potentially being responsible'. Coleen felt sick after reading messages between Rebekah and her agent referencing her dead sister';

Wayne Rooney's mother messaged Coleen 'because press had been knocking at their house to see whether they had any comment about Becky leaking stories about me'.

In her written statement Coleen commented: 'I always got the impression that no topic was ever really off the table as far as Becky was concerned.' She also listed in her statement a 'desire to be famous' as one of the reasons that Becks Instagram account stood out for her. 'In addition to the sheer volume of exclusives Becky had done with *The Sun* and how the nature of them suggested very close links to the newspaper and journalists, I also considered Becky's personality and her rise to fame,' she wrote. 'Because of her extensive appearances in the tabloid press, her column in *The Sun* during Euro 2016 and her appearance on I'm A Celebrity whilst still relatively unknown, Becky certainly stuck out to me as being someone who actively wanted to be famous.'

In her witness statement, Coleen added she had made two warning posts and temporarily removed Rebekah from her account 'but nothing had worked'. She continued: 'I wanted to catch the account responsible 'red-handed' as it were and so I came up with a plan.' Describing her plan, Coleen said: 'I decided that I would invent and fabricate a story, limit accessibility in such a way so that it was only Becky's Instagram account that could view it, upload it to Instagram via Instagram Stories for a period of 24 hours so that it was only 'Seen By' Becky's Instagram account and then I would wait and see whether my fabricated/invented story, which had only been seen by Becky's Instagram account, appeared in *The Sun*.'

She added: 'For the avoidance of any doubt, I did not mention this plan or the content of the sting operation to anyone or discuss it with any person at any time. Nobody knew the detail of what was going on apart from me. It killed me not telling anyone about it but I managed it.'

Coleen became suspicious of Becks as she would 'regularly' message Coleen when there was press coverage of her. Saying Rebekah was 'not in my circle', Coleen said: 'I felt like when she contacted me it was to try and get information out of me.' Becks tried to convince Coleen that journalists had hacked her private Instagram account.

Becks messages to her came 'when something not nice was going on in my personal life', Coleen claimed. She said Becks messages were 'generally nice', but added that 'towards the end its was a bit unusual'. 'Someone who was not that close to me... constantly checking in with me all the time,' Coleen said.

Speaking about their history together, Coleen said the first contact the pair had was when she and her husband were invited to the Vardys wedding in May 2016. She said: 'We couldn't make it. It was a busy time of the year. I sent a gift and Rebekah replied saying 'thank you'. She was unable to go as it was a 'busy time' at the end of the season.

Coleen claimed Becks 'leaked details of Wayne being caught drink-driving with a woman he met in a bar'. It was an indiscretion too far for Coleen that nearly ended their marriage. It was the first time that Coleen had revealed how close she had come to walking out on her errant husband. Coleen described to the court how she split from Wayne after one of one too many indiscretions and feared her marriage may have been over after her husband was caught drink driving with former office worker Laura Simpson in 2017. Her sensational disclosure came as she discussed 'the pyjama post' which she shared at the end of 2017. It was an image of her and three of her children (she was pregnant with her fourth child at the time) wearing matching polka dot pyjamas in the family bed. But on her private account she shared another image showing husband Wayne in the bed. She explained when she saw a story she believed was based on the post, it upset her.

Coleen told the High Court: 'I was in a vulnerable situation – there had been some wrongdoing by my husband. I was spending a lot of time at my parents' house. I didn't know how my marriage was going to work out. Me and Wayne were trying to figure out our relationship and where we were going. But I didn't want the public to know that – I know how quick the papers are to jump onto things. I hadn't settled on: ''This is it, we are getting back together''.'

She also said that when she and Wayne moved to the US she was homesick and 'cried every night and couldn't do Facetime with my parents – it was horrific.' She added it was the first time she had moved 'more than 45 minutes up the road' from her family and said her parents had helped the couple enormously bringing up her children.

The news story about Wayne's drink-driving 'quoted Coleen's Instagram caption word-for-word'. Coleen's' attempts to patch things up after the drink-driving arrest were also made public.

Coleen and Wayne's attempts to patch things up after the drink-driving arrest were also made public for the first time. An article in *The Sun* claimed Wayne had been forgiven for his night out with Laura Simpson after being 'allowed back into the marital bed by Coleen'. The article on November 1, 2017 told how 'the shamed footballer has been reunited with wife for the first time at home.' It said Coleen had shown a photo to friends of Wayne cuddling up to their three sons Kai, Klay and Kit and wearing matching pyjamas as the family celebrated Halloween together. Coleen published the image on her private Instagram account but only showed one of herself and her sons on her public account. Coleen wrote in her statement to the court: 'Whilst I was comfortable enough to upload the photograph of Wayne to my private Instagram account, I made a conscious decision not to upload the photograph with him in to my

Twitter account or to my public Instagram account because of the difficulties between us at the time.'

Coleen told how she was 'really shocked and disappointed' that there had been another leak from her private Instagram account. She said that in response she took a screenshot of a section of the article with the caption: 'The GRASS strikes again!!!....I put that picture on wondering if it would appear in that HORRIBLE newspaper ...You're accepted as one of my friends if you really needed the money that bad you could have always just asked instead of being SLY!!!'.

While painful for Coleen, it was excruciating for Wayne who had wanted the Vardy case resolved out of court, and Coleen had tried, numerous times, to do just that. Coleen told the court that she had offered Becks 'three olive branches' to end their legal war but her efforts were 'in vain'.

Becks lawyer Hugh Tomlinson QC asked her what she wanted to achieve from her Instagram 'expose'. 'I wasn't achieving anything,' she said, adding: 'What I wanted was to stop the person who was leaking my private information to *The Sun*.'

Coleen was 'surprised' by 'how much interest' her social media post caused. 'Obviously it was going to get picked up by the media,' she said, explaining that her life had been covered by the media for the last 20 years 'no matter how big or small' something was. Coleen insisted she did not make her post to direct trolls at Rebekah. She said: 'No, that's not my intention at all. I wouldn't ever, it's not in my nature to cause abuse or trolling in any way at all.'

When asked if she would have tried to mitigate any abuse with a post, she replied: 'Maybe I would have liked to have said that but I have never been in a court, I have never been in a legal case before, this is the first time I have gone under instruction of my legal team.'

Coleen described her decision to remove Rebekah from her private Instagram account after a story about her car being damaged was leaked to *The Sun*. She had given out warnings 'many times', but 'it didn't stop'. 'This was my last resort,' she said. Last resort? Was that Barbados, Ibiza, Mexico, San Tropez? There was so much material for both parties to be ridiculed for in the media. Over and over again, they tripped themselves up faced with expert cross examination.

Coleen provoked laughter at several moments during the cross-examination. 'To be honest with you…' she said, before stopping herself and adding: 'Sorry to be using that.' It came after her lawyer told Becks the day before he'd 'rather you'd be honest since you're in the witness stand' when she said the same thing.

In another exchange, Mr Tomlinson suggested to Coleen that Becks agent, Caroline

Watt, had abused her trust by allegedly leaking stories she accessing her client's Instagram. The barrister said: 'It's not nice when people abuse that trust, is it Mrs Rooney?'

'No, it's sad,' she replied, tilting her head and looking at Becks.

Mrs Rooney claimed that Vardy would 'regularly' message Coleen when there was coverage about her to 'fish' for information'. Coleen was 'glad' no one else now has to worry about 'Becky' leaking stories to the Press. Although Coleen did admit she can't always be sure the other WAG Instagram followers won't leak stories. Asked by Mr Tomlinson if she had a 'large loyal following' on social media, Coleen replies: 'I have a large following, yes, loyal I'm not too sure about'.

Leaks about Coleen's life 'strained her relationships with fellow WAGs and those close to me who thought that I suspected them as potentially being responsible', the court heard. In her written statement, Coleen wrote: 'I would get people coming up to me to say things like "I hope you know that it isn't me" or "I hope you know that I would never do that to you". It was horrible having friends think that they were under the microscope and needed to explain themselves. I recall having such conversations with close friends who I have known for years. No doubt there would be countless others who felt in a similar position but were too embarrassed to bring it up with me direct. '

She said Shauna Muamba - the wife of former Premier League player Fabrice Muamba -
who she described as 'a friend who I have known
for years' messaged her because 'she was worried that I suspected it was her.'

Coleen said she has 'always been confident in
the truth' of her viral post accusing Rebekah of
leaking her private information to *The Sun*. She
wrote in her witness statement: 'I have always
been confident in the truth of what I posted on
October 9 2019 and the documentation which
Becky has disclosed as part of these proceedings, in particular her WhatsApp conversations
with her agent Caroline Watt, has only further
reinforced my view on that.' Coleen continued:
'Friends and family are the most important to me
and it was messing with my head that someone
who I trusted was doing this to me. It annoyed
and hurt me. It even messed with my friends and
family because they felt like I suspected them of
being responsible.'

As for Rebekah Vardy's antics at England
tournaments - there were more fascinating dis-
closures of how some WAGs will go to be in the
limelight, to share the reflected glory of their
football hubbies, and to push their way to the
front of the attention. It was claimed that Mrs
Vardy, 'deliberately sat behind Coleen at Euros
2016 football game to boost her fame'. Coleen
felt Becks 'always stuck out as someone who

wanted to be famous' and 'was trying too hard to
be friendly'. WAGs 'commonly stage paparazzi
shots in order to be in the limelight'.

Becks alleged Secret Wag column ended
'abruptly' after the bombshell Wagatha Christie
post and it emerged Vardy 'got into a spat
with Sarah Harding after she was caught going through the Girls Aloud singer's handbag'
at the National Television Awards. The story,
published in several tabloid newspapers at the
time, was mentioned by Coleen in written documents she submitted to the High Court. Coleen
claimed: 'She got in a spat with former Girls
Aloud group member Sarah Harding during
the 2018 event because Sarah apparently caught
Becky taking photographs of the contents of
Sarah's handbag when Sarah had dropped it on
the floor. Their dispute subsequently appeared
in *The Sun.*'

Becks is said to have 'come to blows' with
Sarah hours after the NTAs had been broadcast on ITV. According to an article published
at the time in *The Mirror*, Harding accused Mrs
Vardy of taking 'sneaky pictures' of her, spark-
ing a 'heated' row between the pair that caused
a 'huge scene'. Sarah had dropped her bag spilling the contents on the floor and as she picked
up her belongings she saw a camera flash and
Rebekah standing nearby with her phone in her
hand. The singer accused Mrs Vardy of taking
sly pictures of her while she was scrambling

around collecting her things. Becks insisted that hadn't been the case, offering to show Sarah her phone, before demanding an apology. Rebekah insisted she hadn't even been using her phone. Friends intervened because they were getting heated.' Sarah died on September 5 2021 after being diagnosed with advanced breast cancer.

Mrs Vardy is said to have 'deliberately sat behind at Euros 2016 to boost her fame'. In her witness statement, Mrs Rooney described the incident where there was 'a commotion' during the match in France when she claimed Rebekah moved seats to ensure she was sitting behind her. She said husband Wayne's agent Paul Stretford 'mentioned to me in passing after the game that there had been some commotion because Becky had decided to sit in different seats to those allocated to her and the seats which she had decided to sit in were directly behind me'. Coleen said: 'In the days following the game there were photos of me and Becky watching the game. Becky then mentioned me in her column in her Euro 2016 diary for *The Sun*. I believe that the reason for this was that Becky deliberately sat herself behind me, even though they were not her allocated seats, to try and guarantee her appearance in the media and I recall subsequently speaking to one of the FA staff about the matter sometime later and she confirmed that to be the case. I recall Becky trying to smooth things over on WhatsApp with me following Euro 2016 but this incident had stuck in my mind.'

Coleen described Rebekah as fame-hungry saying she 'tried too hard' to be friends with the fellow footballer's wife. 'Because of her extensive appearances in the tabloid press, her column in *The Sun* during Euro 2016 and her appearance on I'm A Celebrity whilst still relatively unknown, Becky certainly stuck out to me as being someone who actively wanted to be famous. Becky and I had never had an issue with one another, as far as I was aware. We got on fine, but I did gradually feel like she was very keen to be friendly with me and she was trying too hard and it was a bit too much. To this day, the only time I spoke to Becky on the phone was after the post on October 9 2019 and we have never met up just the two of us or anything like that, although we have been at some football games, or football-related events, as part of a bigger group.'

Coleen said WAGs 'commonly stage paparazzi shots with agencies' in order to be in the 'limelight'. The claim came after 'Becks' and her publicist Caroline Watt were accused of secretly organising a paparazzi photo with fellow WAGs outside a restaurant in Russia during the 2018 World Cup. In her witness statement, Coleen said: 'I have been involved in football circles for around 20 years. I've come across different types of footballers' partners, some of them enjoy and seek the limelight and work on it, others get brought into it because of the high-profile nature of their partner. I know from my experience in the media that a common tactic of those who want to be famous is that they will stage paparazzi shots with agencies. Those shots will then be sold to the tabloid press and the individual in question will split the monies earned from the tabloid press with the paparazzi agent or they will get other benefits such as being able to help control their image in the press.'

Rebekah's alleged Secret Wag column ended 'abruptly' after Coleen made her bombshell Wagatha Christie post. In her written statement, Coleen claimed: 'Following the post, the Secret WAG column only released a further three articles - two of which had no doubt already been prepared prior to my post - and came to an abrupt end. One was about footballer manager Jose Mourinho, another was about Georgina Cleverley and one was about my dispute with Becky. The Secret WAG article about my dispute with Becky began with the wording 'OMG! HOW could she!!?? Coleen Rooney has created the biggest WAG fallout since Nicola McLean whipped off her 32FF superbra'.'

Coleen was glad she has 'put an end' to the leaking of information she alleges Rebekah carried out. In her witness statement, she wrote: 'I should add that my concerns went beyond my own posts. I knew that I could not be the only one whose trust was being abused by the culprit and I now know from having seen the WhatsApp exchanges between Becky and Caroline that Becky was leaking information about a whole range of other people too. I thought whoever was doing this was probably betraying other people in this way too.'

Coleen added: 'There have been no leaks of posts from my account since. No doubt similar behaviour by Becky was also a real worry for many others too. I am glad I have put an end to it.'

Coleen also told the High Court that she can't always be sure the other WAGs who follow her private Instagram account won't leak stories to the Press. Mr Tomlinson highlighted that the more than 300 followers of Coleen's private account included WAGs as well as family and friends. Coleen said of the account: 'When I've accepted people on to the account I've accepted them because I do have trust in them. But this whole process has proved that it can't always be true.'

Mr Tomlinson said: 'You hope and expect that people who have access to your private Instagram account will keep its contents away from the press but you can't guarantee it.'

'No,' Coleen said.

'You can't be sure,' Mr Tomlinson added, with Coleen replying: 'No you can't.'

Wayne's mother Jeanette messaged Coleen 'because press had been knocking at their house to see whether they had any comment about Becky leaking stories about me', the court heard. Coleen said: 'Jeanette explained that she had no idea what was going on because she didn't know anything about Becky leaking information about me. I told Jeanette that it had been going for ages but I hadn't been able to say anything previously because I had been trying to catch out the person responsible.'

Becks tried to convince Coleen that journalists had hacked her private Instagram account, according to court documents. In her written statement, Coleen described a WhatsApp exchange with Rebekah which she said was 'peculiar'. It began when Rebekah sent her a message at 2.36pm saying: 'Omg wtf is wrong with people! Why have they taken that one of you and the kids and not of Wayne in bed! That would have been an even better story in their eyes… d***heads! Hope you are OK'. Rebekah then said: 'That is so bad! And *The Sun* of all people as well! Have you been through all your followers? No one with any celeb mag links? What about being hacked? I would be chomping if that was me! Not on at all'. Coleen replied: 'Yeh been through all but can't remember in point anyone. Got a few people onto it trying to source but if there getting the info there not going to tell. Had things like this in the past and never got to find out.' Rebekah texted: 'Yeah that's true! You don't think the paper has hacked your account do you?' Coleen said: 'No very much doubt it'.

*

NICOLA McLean defended close pal Rebekah Vardy. The former model found it hard to understand why Coleen was so upset by trivial stories she thinks were leaked by 'Becks' but her friend wants to "clear her name". Speaking on Good Morning Britain, Nicola, who is married to footballer Tom Williams, said: 'It's common practice in the celeb industry to leak stories. So many people do it. I think I found it quite hard to understand [why Coleen was so upset]. The stories Coleen seemingly has a problem really didn't seem like a big deal. But I suppose Coleen she is a very family-orientated woman. She used to be quite public but she has been private for a long time and when she took to the stand on Friday she said that at this time, things weren't going well in her personal life and it just felt really personal that someone close to her was doing it.'

Nicola added that 'Becks' was adamant it wasn't her who was sharing private information about Coleen to the press. 'She wants to clear her name,' Nicola said. 'It matters to her because she is categorically telling us she didn't.' She added, 'I'm not here to be solely team Becky, but Coleen put that statement out and Rebekah was pregnant. I saw all the awful messages to her and I saw how much she was struggling mentally. She thought she was going to lose the baby at one point. That part of her pregnancy and the newborn stage, she lost. And Coleen has lost because she doesn't want her marriage dragged up again. They're both already losing, but I really understand why they want the truth.'

WEEK TWO, DAY FIVE

Coleen arrived at the Royal Courts of Justice in central London ahead of the start of the fifth day again accompanied by Wayne. She wore a grey jacket and trousers with a black top. They stepped out of a silver Mercedes and were met by a crowd of photographers before entering the building. Rebekah Vardy arrived at the court in a black Mercedes moments later, wearing a £1,420 yellow tweed jacket and £2,095 skirt from Alessandra Rich, she walked past the waiting crowd of photographers and journalists. They arrived at the High Court within minutes of each other as the trial entered its second week. Coleen once again went for the thrifty option and recycled a Kooples trouser suit she debuted in March, costing £605, but couldn't resist a splash of WAG bling with a Chanel infinity handle bag costing £3,280.

Coleen continued giving evidence, having said on Friday that she was glad she 'put an end' to Rebekah allegedly leaking other people's information after her bid to catch the person 'betraying' her 'red-handed'.

Coleen was forced to continue to wear a medically approved moon boot after breaking a bone in her foot. She prompted speculation regarding the nature of her injury after she was spotted hobbling around a supermarket in Cheshire in March. Friends confirmed Coleen sustained the injury following an accident at the sprawling new build mansion she shares with Wayne and their four children.

Today's evidence saw Coleen explain how she 'reinstated Rebekah as an Instagram follower then posted "fake" stories to catch the leaker "red-handed"'. Describing the 'sting operation' in her statement, Coleen revealed how she reinstated Rebekah as a follower then posted messages on Instagram Stories, a feature which allows users to make posts that are only accessible for 24 hours. Coleen explained users can limit which of their followers they allow to view the post and a 'Seen By' function shows which accounts have viewed it. Coleen went on to post a string of false stories. They included a fake claim that she was going to go through gender selection treatment in Mexico and that a devastating storm had led to their basement being flooded at their £20million Cheshire home. Rebekah's account viewed Coleen's invented stories which ended up featuring in *The Sun*, it is claimed.

Coleen's suspicions that Rebekah was responsible for leaking stories about her were raised after Mrs Vardy messaged her asking why she had been unfollowed on Instagram as Coleen gave evidence on day five. Mrs Rooney said that 'added to the suspicions that I had' that Mrs V was passing information to the press. She 'told a fib' informing Mrs V she did not know how the unfollowing had happened, but said keeping the real reason secret was important to her sting. At the time, Mrs R was trying to identify which of her followers was leaking information about her to *The Sun*. Mrs R told the court she had posted several general warnings on social media about someone leaking stories, but the person responsible had not come forward. The court heard that Mrs R told Mrs V that she had not realised she had unfollowed her on Instagram and that it might have been one of her children by accident.

Mrs V's barrister Hugh Tomlinson asked: "Why weren't you honest, Mrs Rooney?"

She replied: 'I didn't want to because I had put warning signs out there and Mrs Vardy, or whoever was on her account, never came to me and said 'it was me that has been passing information onto *The Sun*. At that time I didn't think she [Mrs V] would tell the truth anyway, even if I confronted her.'

Mrs R reiterated that the pair were 'not good friends' despite their husbands playing together for England, and that if someone had unfollowed her she 'wouldn't have been that bothered really'. 'I felt it was suspicious. Obviously I had suspicions in other ways, so this just added to the suspicions that I had,' she said.

Mr Tomlinson put it to Mrs R that she had lied in her reply to Mrs V by saying she did not know how the unfollowing had occurred. 'Yes, it was a cover-up for what I was investigating,' Mrs R said. 'I had my suspicions that Mrs Vardy could be doing this from her account and when I received that message it made me realise even more that it was suspicious, and I did tell a fib.'

Mrs R added that while she accepted it might have been someone else with access to Mrs V's account, she believed that Mrs V 'knew all along'.

The 'right thing to do', Mr Tomlinson argued, would have been to tell Mrs V about her suspicions.

'No, I didn't feel that at the time because I didn't feel like she was being truthful to me,' Mrs R responded. 'This person [the leaker] was not paying attention to me giving warnings.' Coleen told the court it was 'quite hard' keeping her investigation to herself, not even telling her husband. 'One thing I don't do is put my troubles or my worries on anyone else,' she said. Asked by Rebekah's barrister Hugh Tomlinson QC why she had not told the former England captain, she replied: 'I don't like to put pressure on anyone until I need to. That's what I've always done. I wanted to do it for myself without telling anyone. There's trust and there's trust. It was quite hard keeping it to myself but I had to do it if I wanted to find out who was doing it to me.'

Coleen wrote in her statement: 'For the avoidance of any doubt I did not mention this plan or the content of the sting operation to anyone or discuss it with any person at any time. Nobody knew the detail of what was going on apart from me. It killed me not telling anyone about it but I managed it.'

She thought she had 'gotten away' with her investigation, without Mrs Vardy knowing about it, but that messages revealed during court proceedings have shown that 'obviously she was on to me'. Rebekah allegedly believed she had 'gotten away with' leaking Coleen's babysitting post to the media, Wayne wife has told the High Court.

Coleen told her publicist Rachel Monk to find out if 'fame hungry' Rebekah Vardy leaked her babysitter Instagram post to the media following an approach from *The Sun* newspaper. She was certain that she was the source of a story about her and Wayne securing a babysitter in March 2019. Coleen had a suspicion it was Rebekah, telling the PR, who she had worked with 'on and off' for years, that she was 'fame hungry' from 'stuff she's done at the World Cup'.

In Russia Rebekah is alleged to have 'orchestrated' a 'staged' photo of fellow WAGS outside a restaurant with the help of her agent

Caroline Watt. It is claimed that 'fame hungry' Rebekah did this in order to 'create attention' and boost her own publicity. The court also heard that Rebekah allegedly christened herself the 'unofficial leader of the WAGs' in an interview with *The Sun* newspaper about the World Cup. She denies the claims.

Asked why she did not delete Rebekah from her Instagram, Coleen said she did not want to 'trap' her, adding: 'I just wanted to find out who was doing this to me.'

'I thought by going public on Instagram and saying someone is doing this to me I thought it would stop,' she said, adding: 'But it continued.'

'This person was not paying attention to me giving warnings,' Coleen said. 'I just wanted to find out who was doing this.'

When asked about her publicist Rachel Monk, Colleen described as somebody who oversees her media projects, and has 'worked on and off with me for years now', she said approaches from the media about stories were typically sent to Monk PR, and later Mark Whittle. A message was read out from Ms Monk, who was alerting Coleen to a story being pursued by *The Sun* regarding Coleen finding a babysitter. Coleen was asked if she believed Rebekah was still leaking stories, despite being unfollowed by Coleen shortly beforehand. She said she didn't know what Rebekah was thinking at the time, but thinks she might have believed she had 'got away with it'.

'We were living in America at the time of the post', she said, 'and babysitters wasn't something she often spoke about.'

The court heard the request from *The Sun* came 10 days after a private Instagram post about the subject.

Mr Tomlinson said the data download, given in evidence, showed Mrs R had posted 50 stories available only to Mrs V's account. He described it as a 'serious and concerted operation'.

Coleen began the sting by posting a message saying she had travelled to Mexico to undergo gender selection treatment. She falsely claimed that, having four sons, she was looking to add a girl to the family. Coleen was alerted to the fact that *The Sun* were to publish one of them - a 'totally untrue' story about her looking into gender-selection treatment - but she said she wanted the newspaper to go ahead so that she had 'evidence'. She claimed 'it wasn't hard' to carry out the sting over a number of months, but that 'it worked for me and I found out which account was doing it at the end of it.'

Coleen used a photo of her niece captioned 'Broody' in her "Wagatha" probe to give Rebekah the false impression that she longed for a baby. She told Rebekah's barrister Hugh Tomlinson that the post was intended to 'catch out' Jamie Vardy's wife. The photographs were of her niece, the court heard, but her family would 'not know what I was doing with them'. She said: 'I have photographs with the little girl but it doesn't say gender selection.'

In August 2019, Rachel Monk told Coleen that the newspaper was planning to write a story on her visiting Mexico over the treatment, with Coleen having published an allegedly fake post about the subject months earlier. 'I wanted the story to run so I had evidence,' Coleen said, adding: 'I didn't want the story out there, I wanted it for my own evidence. It was a story that was out there but it was totally untrue.'

Coleen explained she told Ms Monk to tell the newspaper that she 'can't get hold of me'. As *The Sun* sought a comment on the story, Coleen told the court: 'I just said don't comment... so obviously that means they run it or not, it's up to them. I didn't say no, I didn't say yes.'

Coleen explained that around that time she accepted a friend request from Premiership star Tom Cleverley which is why some stories show they have been viewed by two people - including Rebekah.

Asked if she unblocked her other followers from her story shortly afterwards, Coleen says: 'Yes.' She said this was so she could carry on with her holiday, and post things that she would normally post. Coleen wanted to enjoy her holiday in Mexico with her family.

Coleen 'kept an eye' to see if the false story appeared in *The Sun* but after nothing initially happened she unblocked all her other friends. She said she 'wanted to continue with the holiday and make memories with my family and post messages I usually post'. Coleen said that at the time Instagram was an important way of keeping in touch with family and friends which was difficult as the family were living in the US at the time after Wayne signed for Washington club DC United. She said: 'Because of the time difference Instagram played a big part in my life. It was nice just to see familiar faces in posts.'

A story that Coleen believed was based on the third and final fake post about a flooded basement in her new Cheshire mansion was the trigger for her bombshell Wagatha post the following day, the court heard. In her written statement: 'That evening, on 8 October 2019, I uploaded a post to the Private Instagram Account with a quote which said "Don't play games with a girl who can play better" with the caption "One thing I am not is stupid… much wiser than you think".'

She added: 'By this point (late-evening on 8 October 2019), I had decided that I was going to make an announcement the following morning. I drafted something on pen and paper in the evening ready to be posted the next day. Wayne was in the US at the time so it was just me and the kids in the house. I didn't speak to him about it. On the morning of 9 October 2019, I uploaded a post to my Private Instagram Account which said "after years of my personal Instagram posts getting leaked to *The Sun* newspaper… I've finally cracked it and know exactly who's account it is!!!!"'.

Coleen described the messages between Rebekah and her agent Caroline Watt as 'evil'. Rebekah's barrister Hugh Tomlinson QC said: 'She makes it clear to you that it wasn't her, doesn't she?'

'She says she has zero interest in what's going on in my life, which I believe is totally untrue,' Coleen said. 'She talks about me a lot… so that was a lie,' she added.

Coleen said she had never met or spoken to Ms Watt, commenting on the agent's exchanges with Rebekah: 'The messages that went on between them were just evil. There's no need for it, I've never done anything to them,' Coleen added.

Coleen told the High Court that her Wagatha Christie operation was 'made out [to be] a lot bigger than it actually was'. She was asked about a second 'sting operation' that she launched about four months after the first. She had thought about what she was going to do and was going to see if she got the same account as the first time, but that she again did not tell anyone including Wayne. She posted as usual, so that it would look like she was doing her regular updates on Instagram. Coleen said: 'I found out whose account it was at the end of it. But I feel like in public it has been made out a lot bigger than it actually was, it wasn't hard to do it. But it worked for me and I found out which account was doing it.'

Coleen schooled Rebekah Vardy's QC on how Instagram works. Barrister Hugh Tomlinson repeatedly suggested that a photo taken within Stories automatically saves to the camera roll. He told the High Court:'Once you take a photo live... that is then a photo stored on your phone?'

Coleen responded: 'No, not always.'

Coleen claimed that Rebekah would message her 'when there were tough times going on'. Hugh Tomlinson QC said that Rebekah messaged Coleen following reports of Wayne's arrest for drink driving, when he was caught with another woman in the car. The barrister said it was 'another apparent crisis' in their relationship and that Rooney had been 'misbehaving'. Mr Tomlinson referred to a 'supportive' message sent around that time from Rebekah to Coleen, saying there was 'nothing suspicious' about it.

She told the High Court: 'I already had suspicions ... so as time went on things just seemed to add up. Obviously, having the suspicions that I had, I felt like it was a bit of fishing for information.'

Coleen insisted that she was being a 'genuine woman' when she sent Rebekah a 'congratulations' WhatsApp message about her pregnancy

- despite the fact she already suspected her as 'the grass'.

Mr Tomlinson asked: 'So you knew she was pregnant and going to have her child towards the end of the year and would be potentially in quite a vulnerable state?'

'I was being genuine, as a woman,' Coleen said.

'Even though I had suspicions, I would never, ever wish any harm to someone, these were genuine congratulations.'

Wayne had reportedly 'misbehaved' with a blonde barmaid during a 10-hour bender. Asked if that was the case by Rebekah's barrister Hugh Tomlinson QC, Coleen replied: 'There's been a few unfortunate things that have happened and they have been publicised. It's happened quite a few times and I've dealt with it. We've dealt with it as a couple, as a family. There are a few things that have been publicised over a few years.'

Coleen denied Mr Tomlinson's assertion that she wrote the post as a 'whodunnit' to grab attention. In the post on Instagram, Twitter and Facebook, she wrote: 'I have saved and screenshotted all the original stories which clearly show just one person has viewed them. It's... Rebekah Vardy's account.'

Coleen refused to approach Rebekah before making her bombshell Wagatha Christie post 'because she didn't believe a word that was coming out of her mouth'. Explaining why she made her 'It's… Rebekah Vardy's Account' post instead of contacting Mrs Vardy, she told the court: 'I thought maybe if I did approach her she might twist it and cover it up somehow and might not be truthful so I didn't give her the opportunity.'

Asked about Rebekah's response to the post, she said: 'She said she had zero interest in what was going on in my life which I didn't think was true because she talks about me a lot. So that was a lie. I didn't trust her - I didn't believe her. I did not believe a word that was coming out of her mouth.'

Coleen insisted that she 'hated every minute' of the reaction to her Wagatha Christie post. Calling much of the response to her post 'ridiculous', she accepted she had images on her phone which made light of the matter including references to the Scooby Doo gang 'unmasking a villain' and comparisons with Agatha Christie. But she said she was not 'delighted' with the reaction to the post. Coleen said: 'No I wasn't. I have never craved press attention. I have had it and I have accepted it. I have never drawn attention to myself.'

Coleen also told how she kept tabs on whether stories had been published about her during her investigation by making online checks. She said: 'Sometimes I do Google News and click my name in and articles come up.'

Coleen claimed that she believed that

Rebekah was linked to passing information to *The Sun*'s Secret Wag column. 'I believe it was done in the same way as my Instagram, either Mrs Vardy gives the information herself or through someone else,' she told the court. Coleen accepted Hugh Tomlinson QC's suggestion that the column had previously been 'nice' about her as the 'nicest Wag to fans'. She also confirmed the barrister's suggestion that she thought this was 'a cover' by Mrs Vardy to 'put people off' by 'attacking herself'.

Coleen admitted she was 'spooked' at receiving a legal letter of complaint about a month after the Wagatha Christie post.'I was quite spooked by that, I've never been in a position to be sent a lawyer's letter before,' she told the High Court. 'Any lawyer's letter would be threatening to me, I've never had one before'.

Coleen concluded giving her evidence shortly before the court rose for a lunch break.

PR woman Rachel Monk was sworn in as a witness when the court resumed after lunch. She told the court she had worked with Coleen through her father's company, Monk PR. She had no idea her client was secretly working on her 'Scousetrap' sting operation. Rachel, who has worked with Coleen along with her husband on 'a professional, friendly' basis 'for many, many years', told the High Court how leaks about her private life were causing Coleen 'huge distress'.She said Coleen first raised concerns with her about leaks in March 2019 while the couple were living in the US after Wayne signed for Washington team DC United. Referring to Coleen's Wagatha Christie investigation into Rebekah, she wrote in her witness statement: 'I had no idea that Coleen had been uploading fake stories to her private Instagram account, nor that she had limited access to only Rebekah Vardy's Instagram account, nor that she was going to go public about the matter.'

Coleen instructed her to find out if Rebekah was behind leaks to the media after her 'fake' babysitting post became a story. In her written statement, Rachel Monk said: 'Coleen went on to say that it was "the same person that has been telling *The Sun*". I knew that this was a reference to leaks from Coleen's private Instagram account because of Coleen's earlier tweets in January 2019. Coleen hadn't instructed me to make any comment in response to the "babysitter story" and so, to the best of my recollection, I did not go back to *The Sun* about that specific story. Coleen then confirmed in her message to me that she had a suspicion that it was Rebekah Vardy who was responsible for the leaks and asked me if it was possible for me to discreetly find out who *The Sun*'s source was for the babysitter story; and whether Rebekah Vardy had any links with *The Sun*.' She replied saying it would be very difficult to find out *The Sun*'s source since journalists do not give away their sources for stories.'

Coleen's former PR representative told a journalist from *The Sun* that a story about her client going to a gender selection clinic in Mexico was 'bonkers'. Coleen said in a witness statement that she spoke to a showbiz journalist at *The Sun* called Ellie Henman in August 2019 and was told a story would be running about Coleen going to Mexico for gender selection. Ms Monk said: 'My immediate reaction to hearing of the gender selection story was that it sounded untrue. I think I described it to Ellie as "bonkers". By this point I had worked with Coleen for around 10 years and got to know her well enough to have a feel for what did and didn't fit with who Coleen was.'

The court was also told how Rebekah and her friends almost reduced an FA official to tears after she was 'abused' and told to 'f**k off' during a row over seating at a Euros 2016 match. Former FA family liaison officer Harpreet Robertson told how Rebekah ditched her allocated seats so she could sit behind Coleen for the clash between England and Wales. The court had earlier heard Rebekah sat behind Coleen to 'maximise media attention'. It led to 'a commotion' with members of Rebekah's party and ended up causing security concerns. Harpreet Robertson, a consultant for the Football Supporters' Association who was earlier a family liaison officer for the Football Association, alleged in her witness statement that Rebekah's evidence over this was 'simply untrue'.

Taking questions from Rebekah's barrister Mr Tomlinson, Ms Robertson says the seats 'were not the ones that were allocated'. Asked how she knew Rebekah had chosen to sit behind Coleen rather than in her allocated seats, she told the court: 'Other seats were available so I deduced there was a choice.'

Ms Robertson told the court that she remembered 'seat allocations for matches where there were issues'. Rebekah allegedly did not even appear to be interested in the Euros 2016 match in Jamie scored the first goal in a 2-1 victory. Ms Robertson said 'it appeared' that Rebekah 'wanted to be sat in the seats that were right in the eye line of anyone looking at, or photographing, Coleen.' She continued in her statement: 'Indeed, her behaviour during the game suggested to me that her focus was little or nothing to do with the football match. I remember that Becky was constantly on her phone, often taking selfies and generally showing very little interest in the match itself.'

She said 'it was Rebekah's guests who had 'expressly refused to take the seats that she had been allocated'.

Several WAGS said they were 'unhappy' about Rebekah's 'staged' paparazzi photo opportunity outside a Russian restaurant during the 2018 World Cup, the High Court has heard. Ms Robertson said 'three or four' of the footballers' wives/girlfriends had told the FA official afterwards they were unhappy about the fact the photograph appeared to have been set up. She told the court: 'The view of the group was that the photo had been set up by Mrs Vardy.'

An FA official has claimed that Harry Maguire's agent Kenneth Shepherd gave her a 'tip off' that there were paparazzi being set up to take photos of the WAGs outside a Russian restaurant during the 2018 World Cup. Ms Robertson said: 'Other ladies featured in the photograph also expressed annoyance and dis-satisfaction to me at being set up to be in the photograph orchestrated by Becky. One of the players in the squad told me directly that he was also angry at this set-up as they did not court public attention with their private lives. Similarly, Harry Maguire's then girlfriend, Fern, later expressed her upset to me that she had taken part and commented that she was embar-rassed, wasn't prepared and hadn't expected to be put in that position.'

Rebekah Vardy allegedly had another seat-ing row with the FA for England's World Cup semi-final showdown with Croatia. Rebekah was annoyed after her large party of seven people were placed in a back row seat. It is alleged that Rebekah branded her seat 'unacceptable'. Ms Robertson said: 'I recall that just before kick-off Becky had once again decided she would not sit in the seats allocated to her. All of the category

one seats are good viewing but I would often ro-
tate the "better" seats to keep things fair and this
time it was Becky's turn to sit further back - by
just eight rows. Becky decided to sit a few rows
further forward and when I walked past her to
my seat, she grabbed me to complain that she
was not happy with the seats she had been given.
I explained that there was rotation in use and,
in any event, I had allocated her this seat because Becky had a group of seven with her and
this was the only group of seven seats together
within the allocated section. She dismissed this
explanation and expressed her annoyance and
called it unacceptable.'

Rebekah Vardy left the Royal Courts of
Justice before the end of court, during a short
break in the afternoon. 'Mrs Vardy has had to
leave for an appointment,' her barrister Hugh
Tomlinson QC said, adding she meant no disrespect to the court.

The court was told that Coleen Rooney's
brother was 'shocked' when he read his sister's
October 2019 Wagatha Christie post revealing
her so-called 'sting operation'. Joe McLoughlin
told London's High Court that he helped
Wayne's wife create a 'graphic' of its text shortly
before it was sent. 'It was a shock to me,' he said
in a brief appearance in the witness box. Mr
McLoughlin explained he helped run his sister's
public social media accounts as he worked at
Triple S Group - the sports management com-

pany supporting Wayne Rooney. Asked if he had previously discussed with his sister how she might find out who was leaking her information, he replied: 'No, never'.

Coleen clutched a crucifix as she left court after condemning Beck's 'evil' messages. The silver cross on a chain was just visible in devout Catholic Coleen's hand. Coleen had referred to the toxic string of messages between Rebekah and her agent Caroline Watt, in which Rebekah branded her (Coleen) a 'c***' 'nasty b****', and 'trash'.

'She says she has zero interest in what's going on in my life, which I believe is totally untrue,' Coleen replied. 'She talks about me a lot... so that was a lie,' she added.

Becks 'evil' messages

[06/02/2019, 17:50:27] Caroline: Babe has Coleen unfollowed you???
[06/02/2019, 17:50:54] Bex ❤ : Omg 😔😔😔 I just saw wow x
[06/02/2019, 17:51:04] Bex ❤ : What a ▓▓ x
[06/02/2019, 17:51:10] Bex ❤ : I'm going to message her x
[06/02/2019, 17:51:17] Caroline: I would leave it a while and then in a few weeks message her and ask if you have offended her x
[06/02/2019, 17:51:56] Caroline: I bet because you had that cervical cancer chat in the sun she has unfollowed you x
[06/02/2019, 17:52:05] Bex ❤ : She thinks it's me that's been doing stories on her! Of all the people on her Instagram ffs! Leanne brown etc etc x
[06/02/2019, 17:52:13] Caroline: I know x
[06/02/2019, 17:52:27] Bex ❤ : That ▓▓ needs to get over herself! X

[06/02/2019, 17:59:41] Bex ❤ : What a joke! All I've ever been is nice to her though! Even when Wayne was being a ▓▓ x
[06/02/2019, 17:59:57] Bex ❤ : Stupid cow deserves everything she gets! Hope she gets sold out massively now x
[06/02/2019, 18:00:07] Caroline: Yep. If I was her I would have messaged you first and said 'I think you've done this'
[06/02/2019, 18:00:19] Bex ❤ : She hasn't got the balls x

[08/04/2019, 20:59:16] Bex ❤ : Story.... Danny Drinkwater arrested x

[08/04/2019, 20:59:32] Caroline: For what?

[08/04/2019, 20:59:44] Bex ❤ : Crashed his car drunk with 2 girls in it... both in hospital one with broken ribs x

[08/04/2019, 20:59:52] Caroline: 📱 When?

[08/04/2019, 20:59:53] Bex ❤ : He's only just been let out of the cells x

[08/04/2019, 20:59:57] Bex ❤ : Last night! X

[08/04/2019, 21:00:04] Bex ❤ : I want paying for this x

Texts between Caroline and Vardy in which they discuss Coleen unfollowing Rebekah and Danny Drinkwater's arrest for drink-driving

WEEK TWO; DAY SIX

Coleen returned to the High Court for the sixth day of the Wagatha Christie libel trial wearing a black dress. She was again joined by Wayne, who smiled at the crowd of photographers waiting outside court. Rebekah later arrived accompanied by her husband, Jamie Vardy, for the first time. They stepped out of a black Mercedes and walked past two flanks of photographers. Both were dressed in blue suits. Rebekah continued her Duchess-inspired style as she sported a brand loved by Meghan Markle; wearing a £805 smart navy jacket pair with a matching pair of £300 trousers from Veronica Beard, a US brand which has previously been worn by Meghan Markle. She finished her look with a pair of £295 YSL sunglasses, a significantly more muted outfit, having yesterday opted for a yellow skirt and jacket from Alessandra Rich.

Coleen cut a simple figure in a little black dress for the second day in court this week. However, she couldn't resist a splash of WAG bling with a Chanel bag costing £3,000, her £580 Gucci slippers and £285 Saint Laurent belt.

The Vardys' held hands, something the Romney's had avoided doing, no doubt as Wayne had his hands full with that bag full of paperwork he brought to court each day. The high profile trial didn't seem to be putting Jamie off his stride, if anything, he was banging in the goals, while the court heard…well…banging of another sort! On Sunday night Jamie scored twice to secure Leicester's 5-1 victory over Watford in the Premier League. The week before he had scored two goals to help secure his team Leicester City's 3-0 win over Norwich City. While his missus wore dark glasses, Jamie glared forward, he was clearly not comfortable with this position, but at least he wasn't being played through the middle! That was the role for England's old No 9, Wayne. Jamie took his seat on the left hand side of the court alongside his wife. The Rooney's arrived a few minutes later, with neither former England team-mates acknowledging the other. Gareth Southgate must be delighted he doesn't have to pick them for the next World Cup -their WAGS and all!

The usual overload of pictures were appearing on every media outlet. Poor Peter Andre was also on the pic list, leaving the dominion

Theatre the night before wearing a black t-shirt and black track suit bottoms, giving the thumbs up and signing autographs for fans.

Wayne's cousin Claire Rooney was the first to take the stand facing questions from Rebekah's barrister Hugh Tomlinson QC. Claire allegedly never discussed Coleen's Wagatha Christie sting operation with her before her bombshell 2019 post, the High Court heard. Claire insisted: 'No, I never discussed it [the Wagatha post]' with Wayne's wife Coleen. She insisted that she had been removed as a follower of Coleen's private Instagram account for an unrelated reason.

Rebekah allegedly referred to Wayne's cousin as 'Wayne's chavvy sister' in messages to her publicist Caroline Watt, the High Court heard. Claire, who was said to be 'close' to the couple, said the pair appeared to suggest that she may be the source of leaks from Coleen's private Instagram account.

In her written statement told how she had been provided with an extract of Rebekah's WhatsApp messages with Ms Watt on February 11, 2019. She said: 'In that exchange they appear to be discussing the fact that someone else must also be selling stories on Coleen because a story had appeared in *The Sun* which they say they weren't responsible for. I can see that Caroline Watt suggests "It's probably someone like Wayne's chavvy sister". Wayne doesn't have a sister and so I assume that Caroline Watt is referring to me as Wayne's cousin and because I still have the Rooney surname. I have never met Caroline Watt in my life, nor have I ever spoken to her. I am not aware that Coleen has either. I can confirm that I have never leaked information about Coleen or Wayne, or anyone else for that matter, to the press.'

Coleen's 'fake' Instagram posts about gender selection in Mexico and her 2019 car crash were released in court documents. Coleen publicly claimed that an account behind three fake stories in *The Sun* that she had posted on her personal Instagram account was Rebekah's. One of these 'fake' stories Coleen planted on her Instagram during the sting operation featured her travelling to Mexico for a 'gender selection' procedure. Another was the flooded basement post ultimately used to 'snare Rebekah Vardy' - both of which have now been pictured in court documents today. London's High Court also heard about Coleen's supposed 2019 car crash Instagram post, which has also been pictured.

Wayne Rooney's agent Paul Stretford gave evidence. Wayne told his manager how his wife was 'extremely upset' by leaks of her private information in 2017, two years before her bombshell Wagatha Christie post, the court heard. Wayne's long-standing manager, who worked with him since he was a teenager and helped Coleen design the couple's £30 million mansion, which has been compared to a Morrisons supermarket, told the High Court: 'She was in a place where she wasn't sure who to trust and she was extremely upset about that.' He heard no more about it until Coleen's Wagatha Christie post in 2019. In his written statement he added: 'From memory, I think the leaks were mentioned to me by Wayne at one stage and he said that she was really upset about it and it was playing with her head because she did not know who she could trust. I did not speak about it in any more detail. I certainly did not discuss who might be responsible and had no discussions with Coleen about any suspicions that she might have had at the time - Rebekah Vardy's name was certainly never mentioned to me.'

Stretford allegedly instructed Coleen's PR agent not to help journalists asking about the WAG's 2019 car crash Instagram post. Rebekah's lawyer Hugh Tomlinson QC asked Mr Stretford about a notification he received from *The Sun*, about a story regarding Coleen and a 'minor car crash'. He instructed the Romney's' PR Rachel Monk not to give 'any assistance to *The Sun* in their enquiries', in this case.

Mr Stretford said he 'did not consult' the Rooney's on how to respond because he was already aware of all the information in this incident, which he described as a 'bump' which happened around six weeks prior. Mr Tomlinson asked why he didn't tell Ms Monk to 'tell them the true position'. Mr Stretford said: 'I didn't wish to assist *The Sun* in their quest to stand up a story from wherever they got it from at the time.'

Stretford denied arranging staged paparazzi photos of Coleen to be taken. In his witness statement, Mr Stretford said: 'I understand that Rebekah Vardy has suggested in her correspondence with Simon Boyle, a journalist at *The Sun*, that I have an "army of f****** minions" working for me and for Coleen. This is untrue. I further understand that Caroline Watt and Rebekah Vardy have alleged that I arrange for staged paparazzi shots of Coleen to be taken. Again, this is untrue.'

Mr Stretford said in his witness statement that he 'never got the impression that (Mrs Rooney) is particularly bothered about fame or even putting herself out there'.

Coleen was allegedly more 'stressed' about the newspaper leaks than Wayne's arrest for drunkenness and swearing at Dulles Airport in early 2019. The court heard that a few days before the story appeared in January 2019, Wayne had been arrested in Washington after arriving there on a flight from Saudi Arabia. In his written statement to the court, Wayne's manager: 'At the time, Coleen was very stressed which I wrongly put down to difficulties with coming to terms with how different things were in the US, rather than because of newspaper leaks. My lack of attention to the situation at the time would have been due to upcoming closure of the transfer window.'

Caroline Watt was set up to 'take the blame' for leaking stories. In return, Rebekah had agreed she would' look after' her agent and friend 'behind the scenes', it was claimed. In his written statement, Stretford told of Ms Watt's alleged sacking in the aftermath of Coleen's Wagatha Christie post. Mr Stretford told the court he received a call from PR expert Ian Monk who broke the news of the 'sacking' 'sometime between October 11 and 15 2019. In court documents he said: 'Ian told me that he had been informed that a note had been sent round to all news desks that Rebekah Vardy had sacked Caroline Watt as her agent.' He said any updates or information relating to the matter from then would be coming from Rebekah's solicitors. He added: 'I recall having a discussion with Ian Monk and it was my understanding that there were rumours circulating at the time that Rebekah Vardy was going to be severing ties with Caroline Watt albeit she would look after Caroline Watt behind the scenes in return for her publicly taking the blame for having leaked Coleen's Instagram stories and posts to *The Sun*.'

Coleen is a 'very private person' and the abuse directed at Rebekah was 'absolutely unacceptable'. Stretford said. Although he was aware that Rebekah had received 'absolutely unacceptable' levels of abuse after Coleen's Wagatha Christie 2019 post.

Asked by Coleen's lawyer David Sherborne what type of person Coleen is, Mr Stretford said: 'A very private person.'

Mr Sherborne said: 'Was Mrs Rooney the sort of person who would share her feelings with lots of people?'

Mr Stretford replied: 'Absolutely not.'

*

The three stories posted by Coleen on her private Instagram account as part of her investigation were revealed in court documents today.

As part of the 'sting operation' Coleen Rooney planted three false stories on her private Instagram account, with the viewers restricted to only Rebekah Vardy's account, to see whether they would be leaked to *The Sun* newspaper.

One of these stories was posted on April 8, 2019, with Coleen claiming she was travelling to Mexico to look into a procedure to determine a baby's sex. 'Let's go and see what this gender selection is all about,' Mrs Rooney posted, accompanied with a number of heart emojis.

On January 22, 2019, Coleen Rooney post-ed a picture on her private Instagram, showing damage to her car after a collision. The next day Rebekah Vardy says in a WhatsApp message to Caroline Watt: 'She's a nasty b***h x' and 'I've taken a big dislike to her!... Would love to leak those stories x'. Rebekah claims her comments were not about Coleen.

The post that resulted in a newspaper article headlined 'Wayne and Coleen Rooney's £20mil-lion 'Morrisons mansion' flooded during Storm

Lorenzo'. The court heard that the post, only visible to Rebekah's Instagram account, showed a bottle of wine and was captioned: 'Needed after today… flood in the basement of our new house… when it all seemed to be going so well'

*

Finally, the main man appeared in the witness box. Wayne Rooney stepped off the bench to take centre stage at this sensational trial. The former England captain took to the stand after being called as a witness. He's faced the cameras more times than he has scored goals or after match interviews, but he would have faced nothing like this with former England teammate Jamie Vardy sat just feet away next to wife Rebekah. Before he took to the witness stand, Wayne bumped the table in front of him and Coleen as he sat down, spilling a glass of water all over the surface. Coleen stepped in to mop up her husband's mess and deployed a packet of tissues from her bag.

Wayne swore to tell the truth holding a Bible in his hand. Jamie stared at the laptop in front of him, avoiding eye contact with his former England team-mate at all costs.

Jamie, making his first appearance in the court, was clearly a comfort for his wife, as they sat holding hands with her husband, leaning onto his shoulder with her arm in the crook of his. The couple shared a packet of mints as the evidence progressed and for the first time, Rebekah was seen to smile at one point. On a notepad in front of her, Rebekah doodled flowers and a drawing of a desert island with a palm tree.

Wayne told the court how he was pulled aside and asked by then England manager Roy Hodgson to speak to Jamie Vardy to ask his wife to 'calm down' during the Euro 2016 tournament to avoid her continuing 'causing problems and distractions' for the team. Rooney, giving evidence from the witness box, told the court that he had been asked to speak to Vardy by Hodgson and his then assistant manager Gary Neville. He said: 'They asked me, as captain, would I be able to speak to Mr Vardy on issues regarding his wife and I think we all knew that and I think we all knew we spoke about it. I'd need to speak to Mr Vardy and ask him to speak to his wife and ask him to say to ask his wife to calm down, and not bring any issues off the field that were unnecessary." The court had already heard how Rebekah 'deliberately' chose to swap seats at a match to get closer to Coleen, allegedly in order to boost her own fame. She denies the claim. The Court had also heard that an FA official was nearly 'reduced to tears' when Rebekah's friends told the representative to 'f**k off' when asked to go back to their seats. Rebekah denies the claim.

Wayne described talking to Jamie to ask his wife Rebekah to 'calm down' at the Euros 2016 as 'awkward' for both footballers. When Rooney mentioned the disputed 'calm down' conversation with his former England team-mate, Vardy looked up from the laptop in front of him and shot Wayne a very significant and hostile stare. The frosty looks were going in both directions, with Coleen looking daggers at Rebekah, with the combination of a smirk and a sneer at various points during the morning's hearing.

Hugh Tomlinson QC, for Rebekah, said:

'Ask his wife to calm down? She wasn't dancing on tables.'

Rooney replied: 'No, she wasn't, as far as I'm aware. It was a lot of negativity amongst a lot of media coverage which as a group of players and as the manager of England he didn't want that to happen, so he asked would I be able to speak to Jamie and I went and done so. It was an awkward situation for me and I'm sure it was an awkward situation for Mr Vardy, but I felt it was in the best interests of the team."

Wayne told the Court that the England management feared that Rebekah had 'some kind of column in *The Sun*'. Rooney added: 'I think there was a few things at the time with Rebekah which the leaders of the team asked me to speak to Jamie about. I was at the understanding Rebekah had a column in *The Sun* newspaper and as I state... I obviously had better things on my mind. It was obviously awkward for me.'

Despite their wives' dispute, Wayne would have tried to lure Jamie out of international retirement for Euro 2020 had he been in charge, he wrote in The Times. He said: 'Some people may be surprised at this, especially with the legal case between my wife and Jamie's wife.' An indication that Wayne did know what was going on despite saying he only found out this week, no doubt meaning he only found all the details this week?

Wayne told how Rebekah spent so much

time speaking to her husband on FaceTime during Euro 2016 preparations that it was almost like she was 'almost there with the team'.

Rooney, who was England captain during the tournament, said while teammates were playing darts and pool in their down time, Jamie was speaking to his wife. Rooney said: 'It was spoken amongst the players that no one should have any distractions . We didn't want any newspaper articles or columns. I was asked to speak to Mr Vardy by the England manager, which I did so.'

Rooney said he '100%' spoke to Jamie but did not know if he then spoke to his wife. It wasn't my place to speak to Mrs Vardy,' Rooney said.

Under questioning from Mr Tomlinson, Rooney said he did not remember him and Vardy speaking to a Sun journalist.

'As England captain I would always try and protect the players in public as much as I could,' Rooney said.

Wayne continued 'Jamie was a team-mate for the national team, he's not someone I have ever particularly been friends with on a social level.' He then recalled the 'awkward' conversation with Jamie during the Euros 2016 tournament. 'We were in the games room, there was table tennis. I spoke to him, he had a can of Red Bull and I had a coffee, I remember those details because it was so awkward', he said.

The court heard Rebekah's claim that Jamie was never given such a message - and she has even said that she had raised the matter with Rooney during one of her FaceTime conversations with Vardy at Euro 2016. However, Rooney said he did not recall being next to Vardy when he was having a conversation with Rebekah, in which Rooney is alleged to have denied the conversation took place. And Rooney added that he did not know whether Vardy had told his wife that England manager Roy Hodgson had asked Rooney to speak to Vardy about her.

The Wagatha Christie furore was 'really traumatic' for Coleen, her husband told the High Court. Asked by David Sherborne, his wife's barrister, if he had wanted to be in court for the last six days supporting his wife, Rooney replied: 'I don't think anybody wants to be in court but for me and my wife we don't want to be in court. I've watched my wife over the past two, two and a half years, really struggle with everything that's gone on, she's become a different mother, a different wife. It's been really traumatic for my wife through this situation.'

He adds: 'Hopefully whatever the judgment is... me, my wife, our children can go on and live our lives. This isn't something we wanted to be part of.'

Wayne told the court that he 'didn't want to get involved' when his wife became 'frustrated' at alleged leaks of her information to *The Sun*.

Rooney continued: 'I'm not big on social media and I didn't want to get involved. My wife is an independent woman who does her own thing and I didn't want to get involved in what the situation was.'

Rooney said that social media was the 'least' of his worries amid helping his wife with their four children. 'She made me aware of it and that was the last time I actually spoke about it,' Rooney said.

The court also heard Mr Rooney had never had a personal relationship with any journalist from *The Sun* newspaper. 'Everyone knows the history between Liverpudlians and *The Sun* newspaper,' he said, with reference to the coverage around the Hillsborough disaster. 'I have never spoken to a Sun journalist on a personal level.'

Wayne said that abuse directed at Rebekah was 'disgusting'.He was asked by Hugh Tomlinson QC if he had discussed with his wife the 'very high level of abuse and trolling' that came after her October 2019 'reveal' post. 'Me sitting here in this court room, this trial is the first time I'm hearing almost everything in this case. It's been a long week,' Rooney said. 'I've never discussed it really with my wife. The abuse Mrs Vardy has received, I think, is disgusting. It's not right (for) a woman to receive that abuse. But I never really discussed being part of this, I've been here to support my wife.'

Yet, Coleen allegedly told Wayne she thought 'Becky' Vardy was leaking stories to the media. In his written witness statement, Wayne said: 'In around January 2019, whilst we were living in the US, I recall Coleen again being distressed about the fact that private information that she had uploaded to her private Instagram account was being leaked to *The Sun*. I remember she uploaded something on Twitter to make it clear that she was aware of what was happening and that she was unhappy about it. I think it was around this time that Coleen had mentioned to me that she thought it could be Becky. Again, being the person that I am, I didn't pay a massive amount of attention to it but I hoped that the leaks would stop now that Coleen had gone public and that would be the end of the matter.'

In the court recess Jamie took aim as any top scorer would do and shot down Wayne's claims as 'nonsense' that he was asked to tell his wife to 'calm down' at the Euros 2016. In a statement outside the hearing, the Leicester City player's representatives said: 'Wayne is talking nonsense. He must be confused because he never spoke to me about issues concerning Becky's media work at Euro 2016. There was nothing to speak about, I know this because I discuss everything with Becky.'

When told that Jamie denied he was asked to get Rebekah to 'calm down', Rooney said: 'I'm sat here on oath. I 100 per cent spoke to Mr

Vardy. If he wants to speak that and relay that back to his wife that's entirely his business.'

*

Rebekah and Jamie did not return to court after a short break in the afternoon proceedings. Jamie left grim -faced, but still holding his wife's hand. The reason for the early bath was Rebekah was feeling ill - and one of Rebekah's barristers, Sarah Mansouri, apologised to Mrs Justice Steyn for their absence for the rest of the day, saying they meant 'no disrespect'.

The Rooney's stayed on, though, as proceedings continued, the court heard how Mrs Vardy gave a photographer access to her Instagram account so he could sell stories, as public relations consultant Penelope Addarewa told how she was in a bistro with 'a well known' person who she overheard discussing the matter with photographer Danny Hayward. She said she was 'taken aback' after hearing the 'revelations. Mrs Addarewa said the claim was made during a 10-15 minute conversation which took place in the aftermath of Coleen's bombshell post and the media storm that followed in October 2019. She said: 'They were talking about Coleen and Rebekah and how it's all going off here. Danny said Becky was keeping to her story or words to that effect. He was talking a lot about Becky. He was just so blasé. I was just taken aback. I was really surprised.'

An expert instructed by Rebekah found it 'surprising' that there was an 'absence' of WhatsApp messages between her and agent Caroline Watt after Becks tried to export messages from her device to her solicitors, the High Court was told. Ian Henderson was asked a series of questions in court by Coleen's barrister David Sherborne about Rebekah's data, which the lawyer suggested had been 'deleted' or 'lost'.

Coleen's barrister David Sherborne last week told the court there has been a "widespread and significant destruction or loss of evidence" in the case. Mr Sherborne now put it to the expert that he described the 'absence of this data being caused by the uploading process' as 'somewhat surprising', with Mr Henderson agreed that he remembered saying that. 'Clearly surprised you're saying that was not what you would expect to have happened?' Mr Sherborne added. 'That is correct,' Mr Henderson replied.

Data expert Matthew Blackband was asked to explain the most likely explanation for the loss of WhatsApp messages exchanged by the pair in the days after Coleen's Wagatha Christie post. Coleen's barrister David Sherborne asked investigator: 'What is the most likely explanation for the loss or deletion of that data?'

Mr Blackband says: 'Based on the information that's been provided I would suggest it's a manual deletion.'

Mr Blackband, who is Coleen's expert witness in the case, was asked if there was any evidence that Rebekah's Instagram account was compromised. He said: 'There's no indicators of a compromise.'

Coleen Rooney posted 50 stories on her private Instagram account during her sting operation in the two months before her bombshell 2019 post, included two posts in August 2019 claiming firstly that Coleen's mother was looking after her as she was having trouble with her tonsils. The following day she posted a second message saying: 'My tonsils are gone.'

The hearing was told that Rebekah's 'slow internet connection' may have led to vital data being lost. She claimed WhatsApp messages she exchanged with Caroline Watt were lost when her computer crashed as she tried to export the data. The court heard Rebekah explained that when she tried to 'upload the media' contained in the chats: 'My computer totally crashed and my mobile phone turned off as well.' When she switched them back on the data was gone.'

Sara Mansoori QC, for Rebekah, asked Mr Blackband if 'a malfunction' was a possibility for the lost data as opposed to 'manual deletion'. Mr Blackband said: 'I cannot see how that's possible based on the information I have been provided with the only explanation I can conclude is manual deletion.'

The court heard Coleen also lost data when

she tried to transfer files and there was a computer crash.

An incredible day of revelations over, the Rooney's left court beaming, followed by their legal team, equally beaming. A day for beaming Rooneys but grim faced Vardys who took an early bath at half time. Next day was no training, sorry no more court proceedings, they were all back on Thursday for the closing statements - no doubt Jamie will steer well clear of further embarrassment!

The case was due to finish but went into extra time to allow their respective barristers to prepare their closing speeches to convince the judge about who should win the multi-million pound case.

Wayne was reported to be 'furious' with Jame after the Leicester striker accused him of 'talking nonsense' in the witness box. A source close to Rooney told MailOnline: 'Jamie must have been aware of what Wayne was going to say weeks ago when his wife received all witness statements from Coleen's side. If he really believed what Wayne swore was not true, he should have had the guts to stand up in court and say so on oath as Wayne did. Instead he and Becky left court early and he chose to make his statement outside where he couldn't be held to account for it.' The conversation appears to have occurred shortly before England were knocked out of the tournament by Iceland. A press release by Jamie's PR caused raised eyebrows in the court, which was still sitting, and it remained to be seen whether the judge, Mrs Justice Steyn, would express a view on it when the hearing resumed with closing speeches.

THE CLOSING SPEECHES

T he final day of this blockbuster trial, which had captivated millions with its twists and turns, and even split households into #TeamRooney or #TeamVardy factions, would not disappoint in terms of more tears, accusations and allegations. But there was no smoking gun. David Sherborne, representing Coleen, told judge Mrs Justice Steyn that the case is essentially a 'detective story' and 'like any good detective story, you never find a person standing over the body with a smoking gun'. He said there was 'inference', adding: 'You just have to conclude that it is more likely than not that Mrs Vardy was responsible, either directly or through Ms Watt.'

So many had obsessed over the rivals' expensive court outfits and the often comical court sketches of Wayne, whose drawn likeness has been compared to Lenin, Mike Tyson and even a Maris Piper potato.

Rebekah arrived at the High Court at 10am without her usual trademark sunglasses, wearing a sedate black tailored suit over a bright green top with her hair loose and slicked back. She was not accompanied by her husband. When court proceedings began, neither Coleen nor Wayne were in court as their barrister, David

Sherborne, apologised in court explaining that they had a "long-standing travel arrangement" with their children. Mr Sherborne said this was done on the understanding that Thursday was not going to be a day the court was sitting and they "intend no disrespect". The judge, Mrs Justice Steyn, said: "I don't take offence". The family were given permission from the judge to be absent. The holiday had been timed for the end of the trial, the end of the Championship season, which had seen manager Wayne's Derby County relegated to League One after finishing second from bottom, while pre-season training began in early to mid June.

While Coleen jetted off to the sun to Dubai with Wayne and their sons, it was a dark day for her fierce rival as Rooney's lawyer tore apart her case in the libel trial. Coleen had arrived in an executive people carrier at Manchester Airport earlier that morning with Wayne who was struggling with a trolley laden with three gigantic suitcases and still acting as the bell boy after carrying his wife's handbag into the High Court on five occasions over the course of the trial.

Coleen, dressed in black and carrying a £1,000 Louis Vuitton travel bag monogrammed with her initials 'CR', helped pull her sons' cab-in-sized suitcases as the entered the terminal. Her parents Colette and Tony were also heading to the Gulf with them for a long break. A source told MailOnline: 'It's been a long and grueling

process for both Wayne and Coleen and they
didn't want to disappoint their children.'

Down in London it was tough for poor Becks
as she was hammered mercilessly and was accused of perjury as she 'lied under oath'. The
punishment for perjury in the UK usually ends
in a prison sentence. There are also fines of up
to £10,000. It is triable in a court and the charge
is imprisonment of a term not exceeding sev-
en years, or a fine, or both. In 2011 disgraced
politician Tommy Sheridan was jailed for three
years for perjury. The barrage of accusations
also included an allegation that Becks deleted
incriminating WhatsApp messages as part of
an elaborate cover-up in her fatally flawed libel
action against her rival Coleen that should never have made it to the High Court, as lawyer
David Sherborne claimed her libel action had
'disintegrated' during the week-long trial. Jamie
didn't escape the avalanche of accusations with
Mr Sherborne accusing him of not being willing
to be called as a witness so he could avoid giving
evidence under oath, instead giving a statement
outside accusing Wayne of talking 'nonsense'
about his wife.

The bronzed celebrity barrister began his
closing argument by insisting that Coleen did
not want to come to court for this trial, adding
his client 'was brought here by Mrs Vardy because of the reveal post'.

'More has been made' of her reveal post

than she had expected, he said, and she condemned the trolling of Becks as 'vile' but said claims that she was not the source of the leak are not valid, 'As we have seen, that case has shrunk to almost nothing, if not entirely disintegrated,' he told the High Court.

He added: 'Anyone could be forgiven for wondering how on earth this case has been allowed to get this far. She [Coleen] finds herself at the end of a seven-day libel trial, and for what?'

Becks evidence, he said 'is entirely unreliable' and 'she did secretly pass on information or was prepared to pass on information' about people she knew, 'or was in her sphere'.

Becks is an 'admitted leaker' he added - but the question was whether she knew Caroline Watts, her agent, was also leaking information from her account.

The judge, he said, must decide whether the reveal post is substantially true under section two of the defamation act and whether the Instagram post was a statement on a matter of public interest. 'The issue of truth, is at the heart of the case' and Becks 'abused' her trust as a follower of Coleen by leaking her information to *The Sun*. Mrs Vardy had 'regularly and frequently' leaked to *The Sun* information about a number of people within her sphere, insisted Mr Sherborne. 'We have demonstrated they were regular and frequent,' he said of the leaks. Even if Becks 'approved or condoned' the leaking of information through Caroline Watt, she was still 'responsible for the actions of her agent'.

'Just because she was not the one who pulled the trigger on occasion - because she did not want it coming back on her - does not mean she was not responsible,' he maintained.

A number of witnesses have not given evidence to the court, including some of the journalists who wrote the planted articles. Given the number of witnesses who have not been called 'we have Hamlet not only without the prince but without the rest of the royal court', Mr Sherborne said. The barrister says there were 'a number of extraordinary features of this case, the first is the amount of documents that are not before the court.' The loss of documents was 'substantial' in this case - and was the result of 'deliberate deletion' he insisted. All of the original WhatsApp messages between Becks and her agent Caroline Watts prior to 15 October have 'been lost or deleted', including audio and video. Not only had the media all been deleted but there remained no data at all from the relevant period, save for a single text export. Mrs Vardy claimed that during the process of exporting the files, the videos, text and images 'completely disappeared', Mr Sherborne stressed. However, the only possible explanation for this, he continued, was 'manual deletion by the claimant herself'.

'It's telling in her case this incident wiped

the chat with Ms Watts/ - but not all of the WhatsApp chats with all of her contacts. Mr Sherborne said 'even [Vardy's] own expert' has concluded the way the data has been lost is 'somewhat surprising' and 'there is no plausible explanation for this'. He said the 'only conclusion' the court can reach was that Becks deleted the WhatsApp chat and then 'lied under oath' about it. Mr Sherborne said there was a 'targeted deletion' of messages between Mrs Vardy and Ms Watts from 15 October 2019 to 25 July 2020. They were lost accidentally when she tried to export them onto her laptop. Her other suggestion that a 'new phone' was responsible for the loss of messages is 'wholly unsupported by the evidence' commented Mr Sherborne, with no evidence a new device was used to log in to Instagram. 'If there was no new device, and the experts are agreed that there was not, then the only explanation is manual deletion,' he said, and that Becks deleted the messages to 'cover up the collusion' between her and Ms Watts, claiming they had been 'corrupted' during the exporting process. 'She says the WhatsApp export was carried out on an old laptop which stopped working between October and December 2019 and no longer functions,' said Mr Sherborne.

When Coleen's legal team asked to forensically examine the laptop they were told it had been 'disposed of' because it 'had been damaged beyond repair'. 'No explanation has been given for this deliberate destruction of evidence,' added Mr Sherborne, 'she could not recall when she actually destroyed the laptop but accepted it was after she had been told to preserve everything.' Then, the fact Ms Watt's phone was 'dropped in the North Sea' during a trip to Scotland is 'fishy enough', Mr Sherborne said. 'If Ms Watt's phone had not been destroyed then the claimant's messages (including all media files) would have been accessible. It was therefore necessary for both to be destroyed to properly cover up any wrongdoing and conceal discovery. It was therefore, we say, necessary for both to be destroyed. RIP Ms Watt's phone,' Mr Sherborne added. Mrs Vardy's actions show a 'clear and concerted' attempt to conceal evidence, said Mr Sherborne, with a 'deliberate trail of destruction'.

Rebekah Vardy left the courtroom at this point, although she remained in the building. She left the room with a laptop in hand about half an hour after the hearing started. She returned with a bottle of Lucozade an hour later.

In her absence Mr Sherborne said there was an absence of key witnesses, with neither Ms Watts, Mr Halls or Ms Brookbanks (the journalists who wrote the leaked articles) having come to give evidence. He claimed that Ms Watt's withdrawal of her written statement before the start of the trial, in which she denied being involved in leaking, demonstrated that 'she knew she was going to be found to have lied if her evidence was tested'.

Jamie Vardy was another key figure who failed to give evidence in court, instead choosing to make a media statement outside rather than have it tested in the courtroom. Mr Sherborne told the court, 'of course, it is not lost on the court that he was willing to give a press statement while not under oath, he was unwilling to give one for these proceedings.' Mr Sherborne said that Beck's lawyers knew from April 1 that Wayne would be giving evidence. He said this makes Rebekah Vardy an 'entirely unreliable witness' and there was an 'increased importance' on credibility in this case. Her evidence is 'ill-considered and lacking in candour', he said with her memory 'appearing to improve and be less selective' as she continued to give evidence.

After she was unfollowed by Mrs Rooney, her immediate reaction to 'being deprived of access' from Coleen's account was to 'try to reduce suspicion by waiting for a period of time, and potentially "say something about Rosie", the defendant's deceased sister in order to inveigle her way back in as a follower', Mr Sherborne added.

He said Becks benefited from 'unparalleled' coverage in *The Sun* because of her close relationship with journalists at the newspaper - including favourable coverage about her boob job, her resting b**** face, and a two-page spread where she was described as the 'First Lady of

Football'.

The court paused for ten minutes, after which Coleen's barrister David Sherborne continued his closing argument although Mrs Vardy did not return to the courtroom.

Becks and her agent, Caroline, socialised with a number of showbiz journalists at the National Television Awards, after which an article was published about Coleen 'crashing' her car. However, Rebekah Vardy distanced herself from the suggestion she talked with *The Sun* journalist Andy Halls - who wrote the article - at the event. 'There is only one reason for seeking to distance themselves from Mr Halls,' Mr Sherborne says. 'That is because, as Ms Watts suggests, the claimant was the person who said at the NTAs that the defendant had crashed the car and this had been within the hearing of both Mr Halls and Ms Watt,' said Mr Sherborne's closing argument. 'The suggestion from the claimant in cross-examination that this was already well known and discussed openly at the NTAs makes no sense, otherwise why would Ms Watt be asking the claimant about this, and seeking the evidence for doing a story about it as she clearly suggests. The word leak comes so easily from Mrs Vardy's mouth. *The Sun* proceeded with the story, despite being told by Coleen's PR that it was 'incorrect'.

Mr Sherborne discussed the admission from Caroline that she was behind the leaking of the car crash story to *The Sun*. After the car crash story appeared, Coleen posted the following tweet:

Coleen Rooney
@ColeenRoo

It's happened several times now over the past couple of years. It's sad to think Someone, who I have accepted to follow me is betraying for either money or to keep a relationship with the press.
4:39 PM · Jan 27, 2019

Ms Watts texted Rebekah shortly after it was posted saying: 'It wasn't someone she trusted. It was me', followed by a laughing emoji. Therefore, Beck's suggestion she was 'unaware' Ms Watts was leaking information to *The Sun* is 'completely unsustainable', commented Coleen's barrister.

Becks then claimed she did not see this message as she was busy bathing her children and watching Gemma Collins on Dancing On Ice at the time. 'The probability of Mrs Vardy being responsible for secretly leaking information is laid bare,' said Mr Sherborne.

After posting about possible gender selection on her story, despite Coleen's PR telling *The Sun* the story was false, the article was published anyway 'because we've got a screenshot'.

'It can be inferred that this was a screenshot

of the gender selection post' taken via Coleen's account, said Mr Sherborne.

In the final post of her sting operation, Coleen posted a picture of a bottle of wine with the word: 'Needed after today... flood in the basement of our new house.'

He said in both these examples, it is 'certainly more than probable' that either Watt or Vardy leaked the information.

On 9 November, Becks sent an image to Caroline, which she said 'make me fume' adding 'can we not leak?' Becks was seeking to leak an article about a girl who had used photoshop 'to make [herself look five sizes smaller]', said Mr Sherborne, although it has not been disclosed who this woman is. 'The contemporaneous messages clearly demonstrate that her intention is to leak information to the press out of annoyance', he added.

It was at this point that Rebekah returned to the courtroom to sit in front of her lawyers.

Mr Sherborne continued to give examples to demonstrate Beck's close relationship with the press, including a leak of information about one of her husband's teammates, Riyad Mahrez, and during the 2018 World Cup. 'The claimant has a long history of setting up fake staged photos,' he said. He was referencing the decision to set up photos that appeared to look candid of her leaving Leicester Maternity Hospital with her fourth child. 'If the claimant admitted setting up a photographer it would be another example of her leaking information with the ultimate aim of publication in the press,' he stressed.

He discussed a staged photo of England's WAGs at the World Cup 2018, which caused upset among a number of the wives and girl-friends. However, 'Mrs Vardy was preoccupied with the idea that the photograph would not be spoiled by one of the girls putting their own photo up on Instagram,' Mr Sherborne said.

Becks previously said she "used the world 'leak' where I probably shouldn't use the word 'leak'," but Mr Sherborne said she has just "dou-bled down on her excuses" in a "feat of linguistic gymnastics". He said she is "deliberately lying" and her contemporaneous messages should be given more weight than her oral evidence.

He referenced messages from Mrs Vardy to her agent in which, when speaking about the Danny Drinkwater leak, she said 'I want paying for this x'. He said: 'This is just another example, as with Mr Andre, where she is trading money for private information.'

Mr Sherborne continued to share examples of times Becks and Caroline leaked information to *The Sun*, in a bid to establish a pattern of her sharing private information about other people with the newspaper.   He discussed the Mr X leak, with Becks initially telling her agent not to give journalist Andy Halls 'the Mr X stuff' as she had concerns he was leaking to Coleen that

Becks was behind the sharing of her personal information. It is clear from the exchange that Becks and Caroline had 'already discussed the leaking of Mr X stuff' and had already decided it would be leaked in the 'usual way'. On 3 March 2019, a 'highly intrusive' article about Mr X first appeared in *The Sun* on Sunday and later the Mail Online. 'Whilst the precise nature of the information which the claimant possessed is unclear, she did say in her evidence that it was possibly about the nature of the private deal agreed between Mr X and his pregnant lover, whose girlfriend was a friend of hers,' Mr Sherborne said. 'Once again she was privy to private information. It is clear from the article that all of those involved did not want the matter to be made public.'

Coleen's barrister calls Becks argument that she 'leaked' information about her own miscarriage 'utterly hopeless'. On 6 August 2019, Becks told Caroline in relation to an unidentified girl: 'She's gone and done it now leak the Maldives stuff x'. The article that later appeared explained Danielle Lloyd had a miscarriage - there is no mention of the Maldives in that article, with the Maldives honeymoon reported on 11 April 2019. Becks claimed she had not leaked anything about Ms Lloyd and said the word 'leak' should mean 'publish an article about her own miscarriage in Closer Magazine'. 'This makes no sense,' Mr Sherborne stressed.

Mr Sherborne said Coleen's evidence was 'measured and reasonable' - in 'stark contrast to Mrs Vardy'. He says he gives the 'final words [of his closing statement] to Mrs Rooney' who previously said, in reference to Ms Watt having access to Becks account: 'I would have checked what the person I had given access to my account was doing and made sure they were doing nothing wrong. The burden lies on us to establish on a balance of probabilities that the post is substantially true. It is what she [Coleen] believed at the time... and it is what she believes even more so now that we have got to the end of the case', Mr Sherborne said.

Rebekah Vardy 'knew perfectly well what Caroline Watt was doing, and she approved it', he stressed. 'Mrs Rooney was right in what she said in her reveal post, and she still is.' He concluded his closing remarks as the court broke for lunch.

*

Hugh Tomlinson delivered his closing speech on behalf of Rebekah Vardy and said she continues to deny being the source of the leak. 'She does not know to this day what happened,' insisted Mr Tomlinson, but he added 'it is possible, she accepts, that the source of the leak was Caroline Watt. Her fundamental position is that she does not know what happened.'

He calls Mr Sherborne's closing argument 'elaborate theories' but admitted that 'she can be criticised'. 'Mrs Rooney may think the way she appeared in *The Sun* and the interviews she gave were distasteful.'

He said claims of Becks sending supportive messages 'in times of crisis' to gain information on Coleen are entirely baseless. 'Mrs Rooney (he meant Mrs Vardy) has obviously made mistakes', insisted Mr Tomlinson and one of those being, 'she trusted someone she shouldn't have' - in reference to her agent Caroline Watt.

Mr Tomlinson has made an accidental "slip of the tongue", in which he initially said "Mrs Rooney has made mistakes" - he apologises to the court for this.

He said she regrets how she spoke in her private conversations: "Had she known these conversations would be made public to the whole world" she would have phrased things differently.

Mr Tomlinson pointed out that Coleen's legal team "studiously avoided" the WhatsApp messages which suggested Becks was not the source of the leak - for example, messages where she discussed stories with her agent and speculated over who had leaked them.

He said Becks also did not want to be in court, but she wanted to be 'vindicated' that she did not leak stories to *The Sun*. 'This is a case of Mrs Vardy and a case about how she has been treated by tens of thousands on social media' - something that 'goes on to this day', he added, saying she has received hateful messages throughout the duration of this trial.

He called accusations that Becks deleted the messages an 'extraordinarily complex conspiracy'.

On 15 October, after returning from Dubai while heavily pregnant, Mr Tomlinson says 'the idea that Vardy sits down, and there is a huge volume of this material... the idea that she sits down and deletes some messages, but not many of the messages relied on by Mr Sherborne, is a remarkable... thing for anybody to do'. He questions why his client would have handpicked the deletion of some messages and not others. 'Why would Mrs Vardy, if she was destroying evidence, do it in that selective and complex way?' He called it a 'conspiracy theory dreamed up by Mr Sherborne and his team'.

Mr Tomlinson pointed to some of the conversations between Caroline and Rebekah, which would not make sense if they had been the source of the leak. In discussion to the gender selection article, on the 16 August 2019, Becks texts: 'I wonder who it is coming from then... bet it's their PR again has to be', adding 'I really can't see anyone being that arsed with selling stories on her'. He says this is not what Becks would have said if she had provided the story - or if she had known that Ms Watt provided it. 'These contemporaneous messages, unless it is suggested... that these have been fabricated and added into the export in some way to deceive for future litigation, these are the exchanges between two people who don't know who is leaking stories - or at least Mrs Vardy doesn't know who is leaking stories,' he argued. These messages, he stressed, showed the 'best' contemporaneous evidence that Becks did not know who was leaking Coleen's stories to the press.

In order to establish her truth defence, Mr Tomlinson said Coleen must prove it is 'substantially true' that: 'Over a period of years Mrs Vardy had regularly and frequently abused her status as a trusted follower of Mrs Rooney's personal Instagram account by secretly informing *The Sun* newspaper of Mrs Rooney's private posts and stories, thereby making public without Mrs Rooney's permission a great deal of information about Mrs Rooney, her friends and family which she did not want made public.' However, he said that there is no 'general charge' to be proved - i.e. Mr Sherborne cannot prove that Becks generally leaked stories about those around her - but he has to prove the 'specific charge' - that Vardy leaked the specific stories Rooney had used to try and catch her out.

'No relevant evidence' could have been given by Jamie Vardy, said Mr Tomlinson, arguing against Mr Sherborne's earlier claims that Jamie's silence should be taken into account. He did not give evidence in court - unlike Wayne - but instead made a statement to the media outside.

He addressed the points made by Mr Sherborne that there were a number of 'silent' witnesses in this case. 'We wanted to call the journalists. The fact that the journalists refused to give evidence, can't be of itself evidence that Mrs Vardy is the source of the stories. All it shows is that Ms Watt was the source of at least one of the stories - that appears to be the inference.' The journalists refused to speak to the court, citing Section 10 of the Contempt of Court Act, which gives them the power to protect their sources.

Becks barrister argued that she did everything she can to get her agent, Ms Watt, before the court, even obtaining a witness statement from her. However, this was withdrawn 'at the eleventh hour' with 'health reasons' given, but Mr Tomlinson said this cannot be held against his client. Caroline made no admissions to the court.

Referring to the laptop that Mr Sherborne alleged was 'destroyed' by Becks in what he described as a 'series of unfortunate events' of lost evidence - Mr Tomlinson said this 'doesn't make sense'. 'If Mrs Vardy is the cynical deleter of evidence that Mr Sherborne makes out', he says a more logical response from her would be to say she threw the laptop out straight away, not wait until it was requested for forensic examination. He said the court has to consider whether throwing away the laptop was the 'concealment of evidence' or the matter of an ordinary course of events, with Becks simply throwing away a broken laptop.

Discussing the phone that was dropped into the North Sea - and claims it was not alleged that Becks threw the phone into the sea in a bid to conceal evidence, or had anything to do with its loss. He said 'we have no way of knowing' if this was done to destroy evidence or an accident. 'Mrs Vardy doesn't know... and this can't be used against her,' he argued.

It was "undisputed" that Becks attended the National Television Awards - but rather than being the source of a story about Coleen's car crash, she says it was being "openly discussed".

'If you have got a situation where something is being talked about in the presence of journalists, it's a whole different scenario,' he said. The fact that Becks had not leaked the private post to *The Sun* is further confirmed by her outrage in her private messages to Ms Watt in which she said: 'Someone on her Instagram regularly sells her stories though'.

Mr Tomlinson argued that this was obviously not the comment made by the person who was doing it, or to the person they know was doing it.

Because of the way the disclosure process has worked - disclosed are all the pages where she is mentioned. He said Coleen was actually only mentioned 'less than 1% of the time' in the two year's worth of WhatsApp chats between Vardy and Ms Watt. Out of 1,200 pages of communications, there are seven pages that contain material relevant to Mrs Rooney. He insisted there was 'very little' discussion about Rooney, and 'we don't have two women who were obsessed with Mrs Rooney'.

The court took a 10 minute break.

'It is possible' Mrs Vardy had heavily and selectively deleted messages but Mr Tomlinson argued 'this is implausible'. 'The obvious suspect' for the leaks is Caroline Watt, he says, but the case against Becks 'only works' if it can be shown she knew about and authorised Watt leaking the stories - but Mr Tomlinson insisted the WhatsApp messages 'point the other way'. He stressed contemporaneous messages, in which Becks speculated about who the source of the leaks could be, 'clearly show she is not responsible' but, he continued, whether it was Ms Watt or not, 'that is not the issue' - the issue is whether Mrs Vardy approved Caroline to leak stories to *The Sun*. Mr Tomlinson said Coleen's legal team were making the argument that 'look at all the terrible things she has done, she must have done this as well', but they cannot link her to these specific stories.

A substantial portion of the cross-examination had been devoted to 'similar fact' or 'propensity' cases that show Rebekah had a habit of secretly passing information about people in her circle. 'If the evidence showed that Mrs Vardy was looking at the private social media accounts of third parties and was leaking information to the newspapers... but here, we are in a completely different situation. We are talking about a series of communications involving various forms of, when it comes down to it, largely tittle-tattle, gossip, a setting up of a photograph. This is a long way removed from the leaking of someone's private Instagram.'

He said there are 'discussions about leaking' but these were not necessarily leaks. From time to time, Becks and Caroline used the language of leaking - but now the judge 'has to decide what they mean by that', and in some case it is just 'lose language' and isn't really about leaking at all. That's a very different scenario than what's been said against them.'

A number of the conversations between Becks and Caroline have an 'innocent explanation', Mr Tomlinson maintained - referencing the conversation about the Maldives, where Becks appeared to be willing to leak information about Danielle Lloyd.

He admits that 'at the other end of the scale' Becks was prepared to leak a story about Danny Drinkwater's car crash, although no leak took place as *The Sun* already had the story. 'They are just gossiping, and they are talking about passing on pieces of gossip,' Mr Tomlinson said. Becks and Carolyn 'understood' that Coleen was putting up fake posts to try and trap people, something they discussed in their messages and therefore, for Becks to have leaked her private posts, she would have been 'reckless in the extreme', insisted Mr Tomlinson.

Coleen's decision to 'publicly shame' Becks led to 'horrific abuse' from social media trolls, her QC told the High Court. Beck's barrister Hugh Tomlinson claimed: 'The publication of the post to millions of readers was, in the circumstances, wholly unfair to Mrs Vardy who should have been given an opportunity to comment and explain her position in advance.' He said as a result Rebekah suffered 'the most horrific abuse'. The abuse included death threats while other trolls said her baby deserved to be 'put in a microwave' and 'put in an incinerator'.

Discussing *The Sun*'s Secret WAG column - there were claims earlier in the trial that Becks was behind this showbiz gossip column. 'There may have been Fleet Street gossip this was Mrs Vardy, but there is really no evidence', Mr Tomlinson said. Stories in the column were 'taken from the public domain, generic, or made up,' he added. The Secret WAG is 'made up by *The Sun*, it's not a real person at all'.

Mr Tomlinson told the court: 'Mrs Vardy sent messages from time to time to Mrs Rooney. Mrs Rooney may have found that surprising but really there was nothing suspicious. She was hardly fishing for news.'

Coleen's Wagatha Christie post was not a matter of public interest, Tomlinson said: 'This is really a falling-out of two individuals over what is essentially a private matter.' He said Coleen was upset when she fired off her post, adding: 'The Whodunnit tone which she must have foreseen would have had a big impact, and did have an enormous impact, we do say it was unreasonable for her to do it in the manner in which she did.'

The defence was conducted in an 'extremely offensive fashion', Mr Tomlinson says. '[Vardy] was cross-examined over a very long period... Mr Sherborne was, I am not suggesting anything improper, he was forceful in his cross-examination of her. She found it very upsetting.'

He discussed compensation Becks may be awarded by the court - if the judge ruled in her favour. Libel damages, he said, cover three things: damage to reputation - and he says serious harm to her reputation has been caused; the element of vindication; compensation for the distress caused by the publication. He was 'not going to bandy figures about', and figures need to be appropriate and proportionate. He insisted, though, his client was 'entitled to an award of substantial libel damages' for the publication of the 'defamatory' claims. Tomlinson said she had been 'forcefully' cross-examined by

Coleen's barrister Mr Sherborne and found the experience 'upsetting'. 'It's been a great burden on her for two and a half years and she was cross-examined in an aggressive fashion over a considerable period of time.'

As the hearing ended and the judge left, without any indication when she would hand down her judgment, a tearful Rebekah turned to her solicitor Charlotte Harris and hugged her.

WORLD OF WAGs

WAGs hogging tabloid headlines is not a phenomena confined to the UK, if anything it's quite tame over here with the occasional twitter spat and oneupmanship. For instance the partner of Juventus ace Paulo Dybala revealed a couple of years ago that she is bisexual and may even prefer women, putting Rebekah and Coleen in the shade when it comes to causing a stir!

Argentine forward Dybala, who may yet arrive in the Premier league, would bring with him to England one of the hottest and most controversial WAGs in Europe. Dybala has been linked with Spurs, Arsenal, Newcastle United and Manchester United over the past few season and has been in a relationship with Oriana Sabatini, 25, for several years. The couple started dating in 2017 and have been together ever since. Paulo and Oriana met while they were at a concert of the American superstar Ariana Grande, as Oriana was the supporting act on the tour. Although they met in 2017, Dybala and Sabatini officially confirmed their relationship in 2018, and on July 25, 2020, they celebrated their two-year anniversary.

Oriana sent tongues wagging after she revealed her plans to get married along with her sexuality. The Argentine model and musician has 5.6 million followers on Instagram and 731 k on Twitter and another 303k followers on YouTube.

Born on April 19, 1996 in Buenos Aires. Oriana's father is a famous Argentinian actor and a businessman, Osvaldo Sabatini, and her mother, Catherine Fulop, is a famous Venezuelan actress, model and a beauty pageant contestant. Oriana has a younger sister, Tiziana. Oriana is niece to the renowned professional tennis player from the 80s Gabriela Sabatini. Oriana graduated high school in her hometown in Argentina. After her graduation, she moved to New York, where she enrolled in university and graduated from New York Film Academy. She began her modelling career at the age of 13 working with a magazine that published her photoshoot with an article about the relationship of Sabatini with her mother. In 2011, she starred in the Uruguayan telenovela *Porque te quiero así*. She portrayed Rocío, the girlfriend of the protagonist of the telenovela. In 2013, at the Kids Choice Awards Argentina, Oriana Sabatini won the award "Revelation" for her role of Azul Medina in the series *Aliados*. In 2014, Oriana continued to play the role of Medina the second season of *Aliados*, winning Favourite Actress in the edition of the Kids Choice Awards Argentina 2014. In 2017, Sabatini was part of the advertising of the brand L'Oréal. In April the same year, she decided that it is time to start her own projects and began her solo career as a singer. She released her first single "Love Me Down Easy", where she sang in English and the song got over seven million views on YouTube. Ever since then she released several songs, which got millions of views on the internet - 'Bad', 'Stay or Run', 'El Último Tango'.

Oriana also has several tattoos, as one of them says "Karma is me". Before she started dating Dybala, she was in a long-term relationship with the actor Julian Serrano. They began to date in 2014, but ended their relationship in 2017. A year after her break-up, Oriana began to date Paulo.

In 2021, Sabatini came out as bisexual. She has shared intimate scenes with other women in a pop video and the Buenos Aires-born WAG finally lifted the lid on her bedroom preferences. Taking part in a Q&A session on Instagram, she was asked: "Are you bisexual?" Oriana replied: "Really? If I have to put a label on myself, I believe that yes, I am." She went further when discussing her private life on an Argentine radio show. Oriana told Agarrate Catalina: "There is nothing more beautiful in life than to feel free. I don't know if I am a lesbian and I like women, or if I am bisexual, but I won't hold any prejudices about it."

Sabatini wants to get married. She said: "I would like to get married and Paulo knows it.

Before becoming a mother, I would like to get married. I believe in the order of steps: courtship, cohabitation, marriage and motherhood. Although we will never have guarantees, I am aware that this last decision is the only one that cannot be turned back and that it should be made with someone who makes us feel safe. In short, with whom we are ready to do anything.

Dybala was left embarrassed by the revelations after he had been axed from the Argentina squad with 'genito-urinary symptoms'. Dybala has won five Serie A titles since joining Juventus from Palermo in 2015.

SHAKIRA

The Colombian-born female singer with the powerful voice is also one of the sexiest performers in the world and married to former Manchester United centre-half Gerard Piqué, who played for Barcelona while Shakira was once a loyal fan of rivals Real Madrid. In protest Real banned her songs from the Bernabeu! In 2010, Shakira performed the theme song of that year's World Cup in South Africa. The Barcelona defender first met Shakira in 2010 during the filming of the World Cup global hit, WakaWaka. The couple has been together since then and has two children together. Shakira is 10 years older than the Spanish football star. The award-winning singer and actress has 71.7 million followers on Instagram, 52.7 million on Twitter and

114 million on Facebook. Her YouTube channel is also very popular, with 35.1 million subscribers. Shakira's 'Waka Waka' (This Time for Africa) was the Official 2010 FIFA World Cup chart-topping hit that raised over $2.5 million for African causes through the worldwide sales of the album and singles. Most of the proceeds from the project – in excess of $2.3m – were designated by Sony Music, the artists featured on the album and FIFA to be contributed to "20 Centres for 2010", the official campaign of the 2010 FIFA World Cup South Africa. The remainder of the proceeds was donated to various other charitable causes within Africa. 'Waka Waka' sold over three million copies all over the world, reaching No1 in 15 markets.

BRUNA MARQUEZINE

Neymar's other half, Bruna Marquezine, is a Brazilian model and actress. She started acting in 1999, taking on roles in the popular TV show *Gente Innocente*. She started advertising for brands when she was only four years old. Popular Brazilian magazine, *VIP*, polled its readers in 2015 on a list of the sexiest women. In 30,000 votes, Bruna won the majority, more than Rihanna! Bruna Marquezine and 27-year-old striker Neymar have known since 2013. However, after five years together they parted in 2018. But three or four times, they have reconnected.

PILAR RUBIO

Pilar Rubio was born in 1978. Her boyfriend is the much younger Sergio Ramos. Pilar Rubio and Sergio Ramos have known each other for six years after he and Spain won the Euro 2012 championship. That same year, there were rumours that Ramos broke up with her to get back with his ex-girlfriend, but neither of them commented on the matter. Pilar Rubio is a television reporter and model despite having four children. Pilar Rubio was voted 'The sexiest woman in the world' twice by *FHM* magazine in 2008 and 2009.

GEORGINA RODRIGUEZ

Cristiano Ronaldo's long standing girlfriend is Georgina Rodriguez. In June 2018, Ronaldo's mother Ms Dolores, who rejected many famous actors and models (Russian Irina Shark is an example), expressed her desire to accept Georgina as the perfect 'Daughter-in-law'. Georgina Rodriguez is from an ordinary background, and has proved an excellent mother for the couple's four children, even though only one of them is her own. The attractive influencer stars in her own show, I am Georgina and has appeared as a contestant on the Masked Singer. Her Instagram account has 36 million followers. In an interview with Forbes, she acknowledged her fame and influence saying, "I am very aware of the influence that networks have, and that is why I always try to act with positive values and respect for others."

SARA CARBONERO

One of the most beautiful football WAGs is Sara Carbonero, a Spanish sports journalist. She was named *FHM* magazine's 'Sexiest Reporter in the World' of 2009. The famous 38-year-old (as of March 2022) was married to former Real Madrid goalkeeper Iker Casillas. Their split in 2013 turned ugly with reports of media harassment. In terms of popularity, her Instagram account has over 3.2 million followers as of March 2022.

PERRIE EDWARDS

Another WAG from girl band Little Mix is Perrie Edwards, married to Alex Oxlade-Chamberlain. The singer, songwriter and luxury clothing brand owner is a mother of one. Her social media presence boasts 14.3 million following on Instagram and 965k on Tiktok.

LEIGH-ANNE

She ranks highly in terms of popularity as the pop star's Instagram account has 8.3 million followers as of March 2022. Leigh-Anne is a member of the British girl group Little Mix, engaged to Andre Gray with whom she has had two children. The couple has been together since 2016 after an unstable relationship with Alex Oxlade-

Chamberlain.

HABs

With the growth of women's football has come the concept of HABs, the partners of female players who watch from the stands. Surely t won't be long before husbands and boyfriends of the star female footballers will be the new entourage at major tournaments. Already there are signs that women are no longer the followers but the trendsetters, and they can be as raunchy, if not more so, than the WAGs.

In fact there is one episode that puts even some of the blokes behaving badly in the shade, and there have been massive headlines generated at one of the biggest clubs in football, none other than Paris St Germain where the women are sorting out the HABs in a big way.

Manager Didier Olle-Nicolle was suspended following allegations of 'inappropriate behaviour', but while that was pretty bad, it was the least of the machinations going on behind the scenes in the women's dressing room. In a statement, the club said that players were exposed to events that, 'if proven', would be 'incompatible' with PSG's 'sporting and human values'. Meetings with players were held after a complaint was made public and Olle-Nicolle was subsequently suspended, pending further investigation. Details of the alleged incident were then reported in *L'Equipe*, the well respected French paper claiming Olle-Nicolle 'put a hand on the buttocks of one of his players', with the coach later apologising to the group for his 'clumsiness'. Olle-Nicolle's suspension was temporary, but PSG were without a manager for their final two games of the season which they needed to win to retain the title. The club said: 'Paris St-Germain is taking this situation seriously and intends to bring to light the reported events and remarks.'

PSG ended Lyon's 14-year dominance at the top of Division 1 Feminine last season but their title defence was riddled with scandals, the biggest centred around midfielder Kheira Hamraoui who was attacked and beaten by two masked men amid rumours of dressing room jealousy involving the new phenomena of HABs. Club and international team-mate Aminata Diallo, who was driving them home from a team meal, was arrested on suspicion of organising the attack, as the players were rivals for the same position. Diallo was questioned for 35 hours but released without charge.

It emerged that the SIM card in Hamraoui's phone was registered to former Barcelona star Eric Abidal, who was Barcelona's sporting director from 2018 to 2020, during which time Hamraoui was with the women's team. Abidal's wife, Hayet, issued a statement through her lawyers claiming her husband had admitted to an affair with Hamraoui and she had begun divorce proceedings. *L'Equipe* released details from the police on how the attack took place; how Diallo drove Hamraoui to and from a team meal in a Toyota Corolla provided by the club, dropping off another player afterwards - Sakina Karchaoui - before the attack began in Chatou, Yvelines. 'My attacker hit me with an iron bar several times. I saw that he was mainly targeting my legs and I was trying to protect myself with my hands,' Hamraoui told police. At that time, I didn't see a weapon. They immediately start yelling: "Open the door! Open the door!" The one on my side grabbed me and pulled me out of the vehicle. He grabbed a rectangular iron bar that he had hidden in his pants or under his sweater. He gave me a first blow from the first moments of the assault to force me out of the cabin. I fell on the road and then on the right side of the road. The scene lasted several minutes, it seemed long to me. Aminata told me it was faster. I think the two individuals fled because cars were coming into the street. They started running in the direction of the traffic. We quickly lost sight of them. I think a car should be waiting for them nearby.'

Hamraoui heard 'you like to sleep with married men' during the assault, a detail confirmed by Diallo who was being 'detained' by the second stranger throughout the attack.

The news of Hamraoui's attack came before a match against Lyon. PSG's request for the game to be postponed was rejected. They were beaten 6-1.

A reconciliation meeting between Hamraoui and Diallo was held by PSG. They agreed they would play together again, but tensions remained high throughout the season. A crisis meeting was held following a training ground bust-up between Hamraoui and Sandy Baltimore. According to French outlet RMC Sport, there was an altercation after Hamraoui made 'negative remarks' to Baltimore during a training drill, with both players having to be separated. Hamraoui is said to have 'complicated relationships' with Baltimore, Marie-Antoinette Katoto and Kadidiatou Diani. A report by The New York Times suggested that Hamraoui accused at least two other team-mates of involvement in her assault, and that she has a strong belief the answers to the case lie within PSG.

Hamraoui also reportedly angered Diani by mentioning her husband as a potential suspect. Diani's husband has not been implicated or questioned by the police, but the PSG forward is said to have confronted Hamraoui about the accusation. Diallo vehemently denied the allegation that she had anything to do with the attack, calling it a 'perfectly artificial dramatisation'. This incident came before the second leg of PSG's Champions League semi-final with Lyon.

Bribery, corruption and murder scandals have rocked football before but when it comes to footballers and their sexual preferences, well, anything is possible. Wayne Rooney is not the only global star to be linked to prostitutes! Real Madrid attacker Karim Benzema, alongside international teammates Sidney Govou and Franck Ribery, were accused of a shameful crime. The three French superstars were suspected to have slept with an underage prostitute. Zahia Deher was just 16 years old at the time, and Ribery once even sponsored her to be flown to Germany. All three players denied that they didn't know her real age and claimed they believed she was over 18. Although Sidney Govou wasn't charged formally, Ribery and Benzema were. However, the prosecutors couldn't get any definite proof the two footballers had any sexual contact with the girl and eventually dropped the case. Zahia also declared that the three men were respectful towards her.

Benzema has reinvented himself as one of the world's top goalscorers, but it is easy to see why he was in the doldrums not so long ago as he was found guilty of conspiring to blackmail a fellow French footballer with a sex tape.

It began in 2015 when Mathieu Valbuena asked a man in Marseille, Axel Angot, to upload the contents of his mobile phone to a new device. Angot found sexually explicit material on the phone. He and another defendant in the trial, Mustapha Zouaoui, were accused of trying to blackmail Valbuena by threatening to make the tape public. Zouaoui told reporters he had shared the tape, but there had never been an attempt to extort money. Valbuena described being approached by another defendant, Younes Houass, who told the court he had warned the player about the issue without asking for money. When the footballer went to the police, they set up a sting operation involving an undercover agent. Prosecutors said another defendant was then brought into the scam - Karim Zenati, who is a childhood friend of Benzema. At this point, Benzema was asked to act as a "middleman" in the scheme, prosecutors said. In October 2015, Benzema approached his fellow France player in his room at the national team's training camp. Benzema said he had merely tried to help his team-mate dispose of the x-rated video, warning him: "Be careful, Math, they're big, big thugs." He then offered to put him touch with someone he could trust - his childhood friend, Zenati. Police were by now tapping their phone calls and recorded Benzema telling his friend: "He's not taking us seriously." Zenati is said to have replied: "We're here to sort it out; if he doesn't want that he'll have to deal with the piranhas."

Giving evidence at the start of the trial, Valbuena said he had never considered handing over money to stop the video getting out.

A judge handed Benzema a one-year suspended jail term and ordered him to pay a €75,000 fine. He was one of five put on trial over an attempt to extort Frenchman Mathieu Valbuena; both players lost their national team places. Benzema always denied the allegations and insisted he was only trying to help Valbuena get rid of the compromising video. Benzema was not present in court in Versailles for the verdict, nor was Valbuena, who played for Greek club Olympiakos. Four of Benzema's co-defendants in the trial were also found guilty, handed jail sentences ranging from 18 months suspended to two-and-a-half years in prison. "The reaction is ultimately an angry one to this judgment which is perfectly contradictory," his lawyer, Sylvain Cormier, told reporters outside court. When delivering the verdict, the judge said Benzema had "implicated himself personally, through subterfuge and lies, to convince his teammate to submit to the blackmail". Benzema made a surprise comeback to the French national team five years after he was exiled from the side when the allegations first surfaced in 2015. Benzema - who is of Algerian descent - has suggested there was an element of racism in the case. Unlike his former teammate, Valbuena has not played for France since the scandal began. Testifying during the trial, Valbuena told the court that football was his life. "I knew if that video got out it would make things difficult with the French team," he said.

Brazilian striker Ronaldo Luís Nazário de Lima was involved in another one of the biggest scandals when he found himself inside a hotel room with three transvestite prostitutes. He claimed he didn't know that the three prostitutes were transvestites until they entered the hotel room, where they then tried to extort him for a huge amount of money for their silence. Ronnie then tried to pay them off but one of the prostitutes tried to blackmail him, the altercation was finally resolved when police intervened. Ronaldo's girlfriend called off their engagement, even though the two later reunited.

A sex scandal was already enough to cause a stir in England, but the two footballers took the act to a whole new level, they shot a number of compromising positions, and the tape also had the two footballers dressed in women's clothing. Former Manchester United and Chelsea goalkeeper Mark Bosnich was filmed being spanked while wearing a skirt. The story would have never gone public had he destroyed the tape, but instead, he chose to throw it in the rubbish, where it was found by a journalist. In 1998 United's Dwight Yorke and Bosnich, with Aston Villa at that time, rigged a house with a hidden camera in order to tape their acts with four women.

United had arguably the greatest womaniser in world football, George Best. The United legend was caught by his then manager Wilf McGuinness while having sex with a prostitute at the team hotel, as United were scheduled to play Leeds in the 1970 FA Cup semi-final later that day. Best was only allowed to play after Sir Matt Busby intervened, and in his, autobiography Best stated that it wasn't the smartest thing to do, as he fell over the ball when he had the chance to score the winner.

Ryan Giggs, was the new Best on the wing for United, and he had his problems off the field with women too. He was one of the most admired footballer in the world, but in 2011 a UK MP named Giggs in parliament after he had taken out an injunction to avoid the news of his affair with reality TV star Imogen Thomas from breaking out in the media. Giggs was then caught in another controversy as his sister-in-law claimed that he had an affair with her for over eight years. Though Giggs managed to save his marriage, the scandal managed to shatter his public image and his relationship with his family.

Stan Collymore played for Liverpool and England, and he was caught in the act of "dogging" by two reporters in 2004. (Dogging is an act of having sex with strangers in parking lots). Married at the time, Collymore's wife accepted his apology, but this was not enough to save his job as a commentator with BBC Five Live. Collymore apologised after he attacked his girlfriend, TV star Ulrika Jonsson, in a Paris bar, the

Auld Alliance bar with Glasgow Rangers star forward Ally McCoist when Collymore turned up demanding that she leave. The argument turned violent and Collymore dragged her to the floor and aimed kicks at her head. She arrived at the bar at around 11pm with McCoist, the pub was packed with Scottish fans and she took refuge behind the bar to escape the crowds where she began to pull pints for fans. It was when she refused to leave that the attack took place. "He dragged her out of the bar into a back room, pushed her to the ground and aimed kicks at her head," an eye witness said. "She was lying on the ground screaming and bar staff then grabbed Collymore and threw him out. He was in a real rage but came back later on to make the peace but then left alone a short while later. Ulrika left 15 minutes later in a chauffeur driven car."

Collymore said in a statement: "A stupid and silly argument had developed throughout the course of the day between myself and Ulrika, someone who I have realised for some time is very special to me. My actions were totally reprehensible, something I am not proud of and finding very difficult to come to terms with. In a fit of petulant temper I struck out at the girl I love and immediately regretted my actions, but by then it was too late."

Collymore was cleared by magistrates of assaulting his former girlfriend Michelle Green, who claimed he struck her during a late-night visit three days before Christmas after they rowed over access to their two-year-old son.

Even the lower league clubs have been involved in sex scandals, notably when Jay Hart, a semi-professional player for Clitheroe FC in the Evo-Stik Division 1 North was caught having sex with an unidentified fan in the dugout after a match at Mossley AFC. Hart was still wearing his kit while participating in the act, and he was fired by the club. His girlfriend Bryony Hibbert, with whom he has two children took to the Clitheroe FC Facebook Page to vent her anger at what she labelled as a "disgusting" act. "Have a bit of decency for the people it's affected, Thank God my kids are too young to read. It's disgusting. I bet their families are far from perfect." she said in a post which was later removed.

Printed in Great Britain
by Amazon

83140835R00129